Marriage Is A Blessing....

.......WHEN IT'S DONE GOD'S WAY

SOARING WINGS PUBLISHING
California

Publisher:
Soaring Wings Publishing
P.O. Box 6035
Moreno Valley, CA 92555
(951) 247-0174

Editor:
Nichole Palmer
E-Mail: soulsisterink@earthlink.net

Front Cover Design and Title Graphic by   2K Graphic

Book layout by Victory Malone
Email : Verymalo@aol.com

ISBN: 0-9761926-0-8

Pat has written a deeply personal, biblical, spiritual, and practical expose on marriage. Her personal experience, testimony, and humor, when added to her biblical knowledge, experience, and practical wisdom, are a blessed combination. This book is not for the cowardly, but for those who can muster the spiritual courage to seek the blessing that God bestows upon marriage, when it is done His way!

Bishop F. Josephus Johnson, II
Presiding Bishop, Beth-El Fellowship of Visionary Churches
Senior Pastor, The House of the Lord (Akron, Ohio)

"Pat Ashley is a gift to the whole Body of Christ; teaching, encouraging, and motivating women to apply biblical truths to experience a fulfilled marriage. No one I know has more spiritually relevant and useful information that can be placed in a message to bless others."

Dr. James L. Morman
Senior Pastor
Christian Tabernacle Church
Southfield, MI

This book strips away all the fantasies about marriage and lays bare a profoundly real love story. When you read this book you will learn how to build a strong marriage and even fight for your marriage with a godly passion.

Terri McFaddin

Marriage Is A Blessing...

Table of Contents

Dedication
Acknowledgments
Forward
Introduction

Dedications

To Vernon, my husband and friend;
to both sets of our parents;
to our three children and their families:
Vernon, Jr., LaVette, and Jevon; and
to couples who are committed until death, whose desire is to
please God and commit themselves to making their marriage
covenant work.

Acknowledgements

There is no way possible to properly acknowledge everyone who has blessed my life. It is clear I am here today because of the ministry of many people. I am amazed at how God takes me, a common person, and does uncommon work through me. I am grateful for the journey. I thank God for loving me, saving me, and giving me a life of purpose. As a retired military wife, I would like to salute every woman who stayed the course and overcame all of the challenges faced due to the adjustments you made to keep a home.

Thank you to my siblings: Carolyn McKnight-Bray for being a sister who has always given me clear and honest counsel. Pastor Lamar McKnight for being a biological brother who is also my spiritual brother who encourages me. John McKnight Jr., for setting a standard of integrity for me. And thank you little sis, Michelle McKnight- Haughton for sharing with me your passion for God and ministry.

Thank you Pennie Ruffin, Sandra Boyd, and Sheila Barnes for being the sisters God gave me. Thank you for being faithful to my family and for growing with me in grace.

I want to thank pastors who God has used to impact my life spiritually: Dr. Carrol Broadfoot, Pastor Charles Campbell, Pastor Rossie Francis, Pastor Sheardon McDaniel, Pastor Demiters Miles, Dr. James Morman, Rev. Roland Ruffin, Pastor Charles Singleton, Pastor Ray Turner, Bishop Kenneth Ulmer, and Dr. Frank Wilson.

I also want to thank godly women who went before me and set an example of what it means to be a virtuous woman: my mother (Julia McKnight), Sheila Authors, Sheila Bailey, Marie Brewington, Lillian Broadfoot, Bam Crawford, Dr, Cynthia James, Elizabeth Luter, Shirley Simmons, Devi Titus, and P. Bunny Wilson.

Thank you also to   Charlyn Singleton, who through the *"God's Woman Conference,"* ushered me into public ministry in 1985. I also must acknowledge Dr. James Dobson who first aired my message on marriage in 1995 on his program *"Family Focus,"* which brought healing to couples across the country.

There are woman who were not only friends, but are spiritual midwives who have been in the trenches with me and have labored in prayer with me over the years. I salute you and thank you: Sandy Beamon, Ola George, Gwendolyn Jackson, Leversie Johnson, Kathy Jones, Terri McFaddin, Loretta Morman (my Barnabas), Sheila Tatum, and Gerri Thompson.

Thank you to my spiritual daughters Tometha Faulk, Theresa Adam McFaddin, Angela Miles, Nathala Stovall, Danielle Robinson, Lanique and Leshanea Ruffin, Kelly Wiggins, and LaVette Williams for your zeal for God and for life. Thank you for your youth that ignites my life. Thank you for your old-woman wisdom that tenderly touches me in my heart and soul. My hope is that you stay the course and become the virtuous women God has ordained for your lives.

A special thank you to Carolyn McKnight-Bray, Arlene Craig, Brenda Lowe, and Camille Tucker for your support with this project. May the Lord bless you!

Terri McFaddin, thank you for all of your encouragement and writer wisdom. Your support has never failed to inspire me. You came in and worked with Nichole and I just when I wanted to let go.

Last but not least, thank you Nichole Palmer for taking on the task of editing this book and coaching me through the process. You went far beyond what was expected of you. Only eternity will reveal how God used you to encourage me and help me give birth to this book. I pray your reward is great because you have been an open door of creativity and healing for me.

FORWARD

By Karen Fuqua

It is not often that one gets an opportunity to write a forward to a book that has the immense potential of becoming the basic handbook for a godly marriage. I recall my first meeting with Pat Ashley at her Tuesday night bible study many years ago. She was a little fireball with an intense love for God's Word. Each week my girlfriend and I would desperately run to her class. The Word spoken through Pat those nights was like water on parched ground. She taught practical principles on how to apply God's Word as it related to marriage.

Pat is a dynamic servant of God. She and her husband, Vernon, have a sincere covenant relationship with God as well as with each other. Because their commitment to God's divine plan for marriage fosters restoration and reconciliation, many broken marriages have been healed through their guidance and care. Under her tutelage, I was challenged to look within myself, pray for spiritual guidance, and embrace God's plan for my marriage. As a result, I am experiencing healing, transformation, and fulfillment in my 24-year-old marriage.

My prayer is that this book will inspire you as much as her teachings continue to inspire me. Over the years, Pat's messages have entered the hearts of her listeners, provoking a deeper commitment to a covenant relationship with God. Now that her lessons have been captured between the pages of this book, I believe she will take you on a glorious journey that overflows with the blessedness of God and His divine plan for marriage. This book initiates a conversation between you and

God. The common threads woven throughout each chapter are the questions: *"Do you love God? Do you want God's will for your life? Are you ready to submit and surrender to His divine plan for your marriage?"* One major quality of this book is the combination of practical truth coupled with a realistic plan to help husbands and wives turn defeat and despair into victory and triumph.

This book *"Marriage Is a Blessing"* contains the living Word of God. You cannot read this book and remain the same. You will keep it as a bedside table reference book that you will continue to read again and again. Don't be fooled by Pat's easygoing manor or disposition. You will find yourself caught up in the pursuit and discovery of *"Marriage Is a Blessing"* This book will be an ointment of healing for many marriages as well as a joyous celebration of God's love.

INTRODUCTION

A Love Letter from Pat and Vernon

Dear Beloved,

This book is the culmination of what we both have learned since we asked God to reign in our hearts and in our marriage. In the beginning of our relationship we didn't think it was possible for our marriage to survive some of the struggles that we went through. But over the years we discovered that nothing is impossible with God. We believe that what God did for our marriage, He can do for yours. If sharing our journey helps even one couple, it will be worth every trial and blessing experienced along the way.

Marriage for us was inevitable. We dated during the sixties, from age 15 to almost 18. In those days when you dated the same person for three years, it was just a matter of, not "if," but "when," you were going to tie the knot. There was never a doubt in our minds that we were right for each other. We enjoyed spending time together — laughing, joking, playing, working, talking — and sometimes we just enjoyed the silence. Getting married felt so right for us.

When we said, "I do", our courtship officially ended. No more long, tender "good nights," spoken on my mother's porch. "Good night" meant climbing into the same bed and turning out the lights. "Good night" meant dealing with one another on a daily basis without a break. If we argued, hurt each other, or wanted to be alone, we had to look at each other. If we felt misunderstood, undervalued, unappreciated, used, abused, or treated unjustly in the way, we had to keep looking at each other. If the kids were underfoot, guess what? You got it. We had to look at each other.

Becoming one flesh meant being with one another twenty-four hours a day, seven days a week, in the midst of every emotion under the sun. Escape was not an option.

However, what was an option was misery. This was something we didn't learn until our marriage was almost beyond salvaging. We almost dumped our marriage because we didn't understand how to be married for the long haul. We loved each other from our own personal wells. But after five years of marriage, our wells were almost dry. It wasn't until after Christ came into our lives that our marriage was resurrected.

How did we do it? We learned to love each other through God's love for us. Marital love should be vertical from God to us, and then horizontal from one heart to another. With God in between us, our marriage became strong and has remained strong for almost thirty-five years.

We have a cartoon drawing of two men trying to get a wooden cart up a hill. One man is pulling the cart, while the other man is pushing the cart. It's a slow process especially since the cart has square wheels. Inside the wooden cart are several round wheels that would fit the cart perfectly. However, neither man stops to change the wheels. Underneath the cartoon is the following caption: *"Misery is optional."* We keep this cartoon to remind ourselves of what our marriage was like without God – four square wheels. The round wheels came when we allowed God's Word to reign in our hearts.

God invented marriage. He also created the tools needed to keep marriage alive and flourishing. However, many married couples walk blindly into marriage because they refuse to read the instruction manual called the Bible. These couples are like the two men with the cart; the instructions are readily available, yet neither spouse takes the time to read the directions.

We were fortunate enough to discover the manual when our marriage looked hopeless. In the years that followed, we've learned how to use God's Word to breathe life into our marriage and to help us through every season and situation we faced as a married couple.

In this book we share our lives, our testimonies, our triumphs, and our mistakes. Hopefully it will show you that living the marriage covenant is both possible and necessary if you truly desire for your marriage to be a blessing. Some of you that will be read this book believe your marriage is over.

Well, let me remind you that with God, nothing is impossible. God has a plan for you – to give you a future and a hope. How do we know? We know, because you picked up this book. By the sheer fact that you are reading this demonstrates to us that there is a sliver of hope still in you. God can use this hope for His glory — if you let Him.

So, take your time digesting the chapters. Each chapter is designed to teach you a different principle needed to rebuild and strengthen your marriage. Once you learn to use the principle, read the next chapter. If you are planning on getting married, we promise that by the end of the book, you will have a new understanding of how marriage really works. If your marriage is on the brink of destruction, we pray that the Lord will breathe new life and hope into your relationship, and that you find yourself committed to loving and living with your spouse the way God always intended.

Love Always,

Vernon and Pat Ashley

Chapter 1
Learning To Love

My husband Vernon was my first love. I fell in love with him before I even knew what love was, or how it worked. It started out as a youthful crush. I was fourteen years old in the ninth grade when I first laid eyes on Vernon. We both lived in Montgomery, Alabama, and one warm Sunday morning when I was leaving church I saw him. He was quiet, and very clean and neat in his appearance. Even though I was only a fourteen, I found him very intriguing.

From that time forward Vernon stayed on my radar. I always saw him at the bus stop heading home from school. He went to Catholic school, so he always wore a black necktie, crisp white shirt, gray slacks, and a maroon blazer — and I mean always. But what fascinated me most was how he managed to stay so clean. I would see him in the morning catching the bus, wearing a crisp white shirt neatly tucked into his pants. What caught my attention was that at three o'clock when school let out, his shirt was still crispy, white, and neatly tucked into his pants.

Most of the other guys would roll off the bus with their shirts hanging outside their pants, their neckties stuffed into their book bags, and their blazers thrown over their shoulders. They would be loud and boisterous, but not Vernon. He would exit the bus looking exactly the way he did when he got on the bus. That impressed me.

For the most part, I saw Vernon in the evenings. I would have to go downtown Montgomery to pay bills for my mother. To get downtown I would have to catch the bus, which was only two doors down from my house. Three miles always from my house, I usually saw Vernon waiting at the bus stop. After watching him for almost a month I developed a little crush on him. Soon, my crush got the better of me, and I decided to make some moves. I wanted to meet him, but in the deep South a young lady couldn't be too forward, so I had to develop a subtle strategy for getting his attention. To get Vernon to notice me, I got the idea that when I had to go downtown for my mother, I would walk the three miles to where he caught the bus. The plan was to catch the bus downtown and possibly catch Vernon at the same time. I figured I just needed to put myself where he would have to see me if I wanted to make a connection.

For two months I walked the three miles once every two weeks to the bus stop that was one block away from where Vernon caught the bus. I would board the bus hoping that I would see him and that our eyes would connect. I figured if I could look him in the eyes, then the seeds of a relationship would be planted in his mind, and we would eventually connect. I even walked the three miles when I didn't have to pay bills, just to catch a glimpse of Vernon. Believe me when I say that I was on a mission.

I wouldn't stand at the same bus stop as Vernon because I didn't want him to think that something was up. I would stand one stop after Vernon's stop and catch the bus with all the other students. When I got the on bus, he would already be seated. My crush was so deep that when I had the opportunity to sit next to him because all the other seats were taken, I couldn't do it. I didn't trust myself. I thought for sure I'd faint or die. Instead of sitting next to him, I stood for the fifteen-minute ride downtown.

Besides the fact that Vernon was quiet and clean, I knew from observing him that he knew how to be friends with girls. There was a young lady who often caught the bus with him, but I could tell that she wasn't his girlfriend. She was just a friend, although I knew he wasn't effeminate. I liked the fact that he had a sister-friend. This was important, you see, because I was looking for more than just a boyfriend; I wanted a boy who knew how to be a friend to a girl.

By the time I turned fifteen and school was almost over, I still hadn't made a connection with Vernon. I told myself that it was going to be another long summer, but I didn't give up — September was coming and my motto was, "Keep hope alive!"

But one day in May, God smiled on me. I was waiting at the bus stop in Vernon's neighborhood — returning home after running an errand for my mother — when I spotted Vernon on the other side of the street walking in my direction. I thought, "This is it! I'm going to make the connection."

Now, please understand I had studied Vernon for months and I knew that he was shy. So, I decided to play the "look and see me" game. As he was coming down the incline toward me, I didn't look at him. I knew that if I didn't look at him, he would look at me. So I waited, and just when he was close enough that I could feel he was looking at me, I turned and looked him straight in his eyes. I didn't smile, nor did I show any facial expression. Our eyes just met. He was obviously embarrassed, and immediately looked away. I began to pray, "Lord, please don't let this bus come until he and I make a connection." Sure enough, when I looked up, Vernon was leaving a neighborhood store. When I saw him, I turned away, and began to play the game again. This time, however, I waited until he was close enough to really see into my eyes. The plan worked perfectly. When I was sure that he was looking straight at me, I turned around and our eyes met. This time there was no denying the connection was made. In fact, I was content enough not to speak to him the rest of the summer because I knew that when September came and he saw me

3

again, he would know exactly who I was, and hopefully, what I was feeling. Believe me when I say, "It's all in the eyes…it's all in the eyes."

After my connection with Vernon, I discovered that a cousin of mine lived in his neighborhood, so I asked her to tell me about him. She told me his name and everything that she knew about him, which I later, replayed in my mind over and over, making myself remember every detail. The next time I saw Vernon was at a summer church revival.

I grew up Baptist, and every church member was required to attend the church revival that took place during the month of June. For the kickoff night I wore my red miniskirt. When my cousin and I walked in the church, to my surprise she spotted Vernon. He was with his mother, which was a little odd considering she was a church member and he was Catholic.

The custom in those days was for the adults to sit on one side of the church and the youth to sit on the other. When I saw Vernon, I decided to sit with the adults because that was where he was sitting. I boldly walked to that side of the church and sat on the bench near Vernon and his mother, I sat where Vernon could get a good look at me. It worked!

When service was over, Vernon hung out with the rest of the youth behind the church at the sweet shop. We didn't have a strong youth program at our church, so we would just congregate at the candy store. My cousin finally introduced us, and as she did, she placed my hand in Vernon's. That was it. We were both hooked.

That evening Vernon and I talked until it was time for everyone to head home. As I got to know him, I discovered that he was more than just a clean, quiet boy. He spoke like an adult. He knew how to ask questions and to find out what was on my mind. He knew how to laugh. He knew how to listen.

4

We used to dream together. As our relationship developed, we would talk about our future. We'd talk about how many kids we wanted, the kind of house we wanted to live in, if we wanted to travel or stay in Montgomery, and what it would feel like to be married. We may have been teen-agers, but we dreamed big dreams for our future — a future with us at the center and our whole lives in front of us waiting to be experienced.

Back then, we had what was called courting days. For Vernon and I, they were Sunday, Wednesday, and Friday. When Vernon first started dating me, he would call me on the phone and come over to visit during the day. My parents liked that because it said that Vernon's motives were pure. He would only sit in the front room or the front yard. He never put me in a position where I would feel uncomfortable. I always felt safe with Vernon. Falling in love with Vernon made me feel safe. There was nothing hard about it. He was the only boy I ever dated and the only man I ever loved. No other man ever intrigued me, impressed me, or befriended me like Vernon did. In my world it was Vernon or bust.

I knew I wanted Vernon to be my husband when I couldn't bear to say goodnight to him at the end of every date. It would seem like just when I got to something good about him or a revelation about us, it was time for him to go. To get him home, I would have to call a taxi. I hated calling the taxi. So I would call instead the number for the correct time — I would listen to the recording while pretending to call him a taxi. When the taxi didn't come, we would have to call back. This always bought me an extra 20 or 30 minutes. Neither Daddy nor Vernon knew I did this. What my dad did know was how I felt about Vernon.

When I was young he used to call me "Tricia." He used to say to my mom when I wasn't around, "Tricia acts like

5

she could eat that boy. And one day she gonna wish she had ate him." Mama would say, "Tricia acts like the sun rises and sets on that young man." I never argued their points because in my mind, they were right. That's exactly how I felt. I may have been a teen-ager, but I was in love — true love. And no one could tell me any different. Two weeks before my 18th birthday Vernon and I got married.

Vernon and I spent our honeymoon at a local hotel in Montgomery. After three blissful days, he shipped out to boot camp for the U.S. Air Force. It was 1970 and the Vietnam War was raging. If you were a healthy young man in America you either joined the military or waited to be drafted. Vernon signed up for the Air Force rather than to be drafted into the U.S. Army. Once he made his choice, I went along for the ride not knowing how his decision would impact my life.

When I say impact, I mean the price you pay to wear a man's wedding ring. The price could be loneliness, lack of affection, financial set backs or in-law troubles. Vernon's choice of careers introduced the fear of death into my life. I was constantly afraid that I would get a call that said he was being shipped off to Vietnam. So I prayed daily that the call wouldn't come. Fortunately, the call never came.

I probably could have handled our lifestyle better if I had stayed in Alabama. But in those days, when you joined the military, you also signed up for a life of mobility. We spent six weeks apart while Vernon completed his basic training. He came back for a month then left for his first assignment in Oregon. By this time I was pregnant with our first child, so I stayed in Alabama with my family until the baby came. I missed Vernon with all my heart, but because I was pregnant, being near my mom and dad was a real source of comfort.

When Vernon finally got settled, he came home to take

his new family back to Oregon so we could be together. As much as I loved my husband and longed to be with him, I was still very young and leaving my family was hard. Little did I know that when we waved goodbye to my parents, I would never live in Montgomery, Alabama again nor would I ever see my family on a consistent basis.

Being away from home and trying to make a home of my own was more than a notion. Montgomery was a small town in the south, and compared to the great northwest, moving to Oregon was like moving to another world. The scenery and weather were different, the neighborhoods and the people were nothing like the slow-paced, close-knit community of Montgomery. Living in Alabama around family and friends kept me sane. Without my small town and my close-knit family members to balance my life I felt lost, confused, and extremely depressed.

Adjusting to military life was difficult at best. Little things would get on my nerves, like making friends and then having to saying goodbye because one of us had to move to the next military assignment in another city or country. I missed not being home for the holidays, graduations, weddings, and family birthdays. Being disconnected from the States and from the people who knew me best drove me deeper into feelings of isolation and loneliness. I might have been able to adjust to my life better if there were older women around the base who could give solid counsel. But most of the women in the military were like me: young and dealing with the same issues. We were like the blind leading the blind, and all we could do was what seemed best to us.

As the war in Vietnam was winding down in 1973, the war raging in my household escalated on a daily basis. By age twenty-one, I learned to tolerate the Air Force though it dictated where, when, and how I lived. I spent the bulk of the day with my two babies, neither of whom could talk. I tried my best to meet my husband's need of coming home to a cheerful wife, a clean house, clean kids, and dinner on the table. I learned to become an expert packer because I moved a total of five times and lived in two countries. I learned not to become attached to material things. I learned how to say "so long." I also learned not to complain. But the pressure was mounting on the inside of me and sometimes I felt like I was coming apart at the seams.

In 1973 Vernon was transferred to Spain, and of course I packed up our two children and followed my husband to his new assignment. Things went from bad to worse after the move. We couldn't drink the water in Spain. So, once a week Vernon carried a 5-gallon jug of water from the military base to our house. We needed the water to cook, brush our teeth, and to drink. We also had to buy butane to light our stoves and heat our homes. The butane man would come once a week. I tried to time our usage of the gas so it would last the entire week. Most of the time my guesswork was accurate, but sometimes I was off and the butane would run out right in the middle of cooking dinner or bathing the kids. Because I couldn't lift the container, Vernon would have to jump in our car and try to catch up with the butane man.

Sometimes on our way back from getting water, I would remember how when I was a girl in Montgomery, I walked three miles out of my way to catch the bus just so I could see Vernon. I would chuckle, and then swallow the memory like bittersweet dark chocolate. I never dreamed that my childish flirtation with Vernon would lead to a life of instability and loneliness. When Vernon and I used to dream about our future together we never saw the hard times or how we would handle them.

Living the military life wore on me. We were

8

accountable to no one and we hadn't stepped foot in a church in years. But we hit the nightclubs and the party scene as much as our schedules would allow. Pretty soon the love that blossomed in me at age fourteen was almost dead. Ironically, it was a letter from home that almost sealed my fate.

The envelope was addressed to me and it was and invitation to my brother's wedding. He was my favorite brother and there was no way that I was going to miss the most important day in his life. Yes! I was finally going home even if it was for a little while. I was at a point where I would have been glad to see my family in the airport lobby for just a few hours if it meant my spirits would be refreshed.

I couldn't wait to tell Vernon about the wedding. I knew he wouldn't be thrilled because the ticket would be a little pricey. But, I just knew he would agree, especially after everything I sacrificed to be a military wife. I felt I had earned the ticket — after all I've never asked him for anything. I had always pulled my weight and stayed with him even when many of the military couples around us were getting divorced. We were still together and that had to mean something to him. Didn't it?

I was full of hope when I asked him for a plane ticket so I could go home. To my surprise, he looked at me with a cold stare and said, "No." That one little word crushed my spirit. His "no" was an end to discussion. It was the end of any consideration. It was a flat and final "no" without any room for a change of heart. I couldn't hide my disappointment. Even when he saw how devastated I was he did not budge. I looked in his eyes and there was nothing there. He was indifferent to me.

The man I fell in love with in the ninth grade no longer existed. My best friend, my first and only lover, the father of my children, the man whom I dreamed would sit in a rocking chair with me on a porch in our old age, did not care about me anymore.

9

"You don't love me?" I thought to myself. "Fine!" I answered in silence. "I don't love you either. I don't care if you're happy, because you don't make me happy. I don't care about the way you feel because you don't care about the way I feel. And guess what? I'm going to stop giving you control over my feelings. I'm going to live my life the way I want to because you're living yours the way you want to. And I'm going to do whatever works for me because I've made a million sacrifices and they didn't mean anything at all to you."My tears dried up instantly. My mind went to autopilot. A stone wall built itself around my heart. And for the first time in seven years, I wanted out.

Years later, when we both came to our senses, Vernon told me how sorry he was for his decision. He had no idea that it would affect me the way that it did. He was young and inexperienced. That decision almost pushed me to end our marriage. Looking back I can see that it was God who kept us together when we couldn't do it ourselves.

CHAPTER 2
Peaceful Surrender

My marriage reached its lowest point when Vernon refused to allow me to attend my brother's wedding. He could have helped me get a free flight on a military transport plane. He could have taken a few days off and gone with me, but he was dead set and determined to have it his way. In today's culture a woman might ask me why I didn't just get a plane ticket and go to my brother's wedding anyway. Why did I let my husband stop me from doing something that was so important to me? Let me explain to you, that thirty years ago, women were not nearly as independent. First of all, I didn't have a job, I was in a foreign country, and I had two young children and no babysitter. In other words, I was stuck!

For one solid year, I had little or nothing to say to Vernon. We only talked about the basics, the children and the house. He would ask me if kids get enough to eat. I would ask him if the bills got paid. Whose turn is it to read the bedtime stories? Can we have meatloaf tonight for dinner? Whose turn is it to bathe the kids? Will you pick up some milk on your way home from work? Is my uniform shirt clean?

Our conversations were never personal. We stopped laughing, sharing, and dreaming together. We talked only when necessary and only in polite tones. We weren't big on arguing, but were very big on telling the truth in a manner that was as bitter and as insensitive as possible. We didn't care if the truth hurt or maimed, just as long as we could look each other in the eye without shame. We tolerated each other for the sake of the kids and only did what was necessary to keep our family going. Vernon was a good provider and he worked two or three jobs to ensure our needs were met. Every payday he gave me what I needed to take care of the house. I in turn took care of the shopping, cooking, cleaning, and caring for the children with vigor. I never let the clothes go unwashed. I never let a meal go uncooked.

Despite of all of our harsh feelings toward one another, our physical intimacy was not lacking. Sometimes when we needed to relax and take a break we would tuck the kids in bed and close our door. But as soon as we stepped over the threshold of our bedroom door the next morning, we'd go back to being roommates. We may have been physically satisfied, but our hearts were filled with discontentment. Sexual intimacy wasn't able to fill the void that we were both experiencing. Many people think that if you have a good sex life then you have a good love life, but Vernon and I were living proof that you can have one without the other.

After "the wedding incident" Vernon and I lived separate lives. When we did have fun, we had it separately. We had separate friends and Saturday night became our party night. I would get dressed and hit the military base looking single and wearing my wedding ring — just the girls and me. Vernon would leave the house with his friends for a night on the town. I would go in one direction and he would go in another. On a few occasions we would go out together, but not too often. Our lifestyle made it clear that our marriage was in trouble, yet we both were committed to making the best out of a bad situation.

We would have probably stayed on that track, but the godly influence of my mother reached across the ocean to make me rethink my lifestyle. She wrote me letters insisting that I take the kids to church. Vernon Jr. and LaVette were only three and four years old at the time, nevertheless Mama insisted that I take them to church. In the four years since Vernon and I married, we had never stepped foot in a church. But somehow Mama's letters began to do a work in my heart.

Finally on a bright Sunday morning in 1974, I got up and dressed the kids. I didn't tell Vernon where I was going only that I'd be back. The children and I made the short trip to the base chapel, which was Protestant. I dropped them off at the Sunday school room and sat in the car until it was over. When little Vernon and LaVette got back in the car they enthusiastically chattered all the way home about what they learned. The next Saturday they asked me if we were going to take them back to church. I just looked at them and wondered how they would know it was a Saturday night and the next day was Sunday. I said, "Yes, we're going back." When Vernon heard me and the children talking about church, he didn't say a word. He just rolled his eyes.

The next morning, I took the kids back to church and once again I sat in the car and waited. But this time my mind wandered back to the memories of when Mama and Daddy would take me to church as a young child. They never sat in the car because they always went to church with us. In fact, my life was centered on church because my father was the chairman of the deacon board and superintendent of the Sunday school. My mother taught Sunday school and was over the youth choir. In all honesty, I had no choice but to go to church and be involved in all the activities provided there.

In light of my background, I knew it was wrong for me to sit in the car when I was only a stone's throw away from hearing the Word of God. I should have been in there with my children, not sitting out here in the hot sun. "What was wrong with me, had I changed that much?" I thought to myself.

This time when Sunday school was over and the kids jumped back in the car, I listened intently to what they learned, savoring their experience. I was excited to hear the songs they learned and to see their drawings of Jesus.

The next Sunday, once again we got dressed and

prepared to leave for church. Vernon just looked at us, grunted, and kept on reading his paper. I ignored him and calmly walked out the door though I understood why he was not impressed with me. We still partied every Saturday. Last night had been no exception. But even still, there was something about church I craved and I wasn't going to stop going until I got it. After I escorted the kids to Sunday school, I went to the adult Sunday school session. Hearing the Word of God again awakened areas in me that I never realized had died.

Now the Word of God that had been deposited in my heart from my childhood was being reactivated. Once I started going every Sunday, I didn't stop at Sunday school; I had become addicted to the Word. Hearing the preached Word reminded me of my old pastor in Montgomery. He would start out slowly teaching the Word but always ended up with loud preaching and pounding passionately on the podium.

In the military base chapel, I would sit mesmerized and completely filled as the Word danced my heart. There was a young man in the congregation who took an interest in me. He was a sweet, sincere guy. He was the only one in the congregation who ever witnessed to me. The first time he did, I instantly felt convicted — only at the time I didn't know how conviction worked. He told me my lifestyle was ungodly. "You can't party on Saturday thinking you're going to get up Sunday morning to praise the Lord. It doesn't work like that. You have to have the mind of Christ," he said.

After I listened to what he had to say I knew it was time for me to make some changes about the way I was living and how I was raising my children. My heart throbbed with the pain of my wrongdoing. His words hurt me because he was telling the truth. I needed to change. I wanted my children to grow up respecting me and their father.

I began to read the Word consistently. I stopped

partying. I stopped meeting the girls for drinks. Instead, I went to Bible study on a weekly basis. One Sunday I went to church and there was a call for anyone who wanted to accept Christ. I walked to the front of the church and gave my heart to the Lord. When I completely surrendered my heart to the Lord, I stood on the brink of a brand new phase of my life.

It's seems strange that I found God in Spain, among a people who didn't speak English, and in an environment where being black was a rarity. Spain had always been my personal hell. I never dreamed that it would one day become my personal piece of heaven.

For five years I had lived my life with Vernon making my own choices and decisions. All I got out of it was heartache and disappointment. My dream of loving Vernon had become a nightmare that I could not wake up from. Even though I had found the Lord, when it came to my marriage, I was sick and tired of being sick and tired.

I didn't love my husband, and I didn't hate him. I wasn't glad to see him come home, and wasn't glad to see him leave. I didn't care what time he came home, or if he came home at all. I had no feelings for him one way other the other. I didn't care and neither did he. We were only in our marriage for our children, and that too was wearing thin.

My marriage was dead, so why should I be married anymore? I prayed and asked God to show me what to do. How could I live my life with a man who felt nothing for me and I didn't feel anything for him? How do I live my life as an example that my children could look up to with pride?

"How do I do this, Lord? How do I do this?"

I missed Vernon. We used to be the best of friends. We could laugh, joke, play, and dream together. I couldn't remember the last time we dreamed about anything. Our marriage was in deep trouble, but neither one of us knew how to turn our relationship around. My only example of how marriage worked came from my parents. Growing up, I knew my parents were deeply committed to each other, but there were times I felt that Daddy disrespected Mama, especially in the way he'd speak to her. Listening to him made me angry because I felt he pushed her around. I felt he didn't appreciate her or the things she did for him, nor did I feel he respected her. I would often say to Mama, "I wouldn't let him talk to *me* like that!"

She'd calmly look me in the eye and answer, "Someone's got to keep the peace in this house. All of us can't go around acting like your daddy." I didn't understand her stance until I heard the same disrespect come out of Vernon's mouth. Only my response wasn't peaceful like Mama's. I was defiant like my father. When Vernon tried to cut me with bitter words, I'd cut him back. I wasn't about to allow him to mistreat me the way I saw my father mistreat my mother.

But as time passed, I was tired of the verbal fights. I needed to find a new way to deal with Vernon. I desperately wanted a new lifestyle. Not knowing what to do, I kept reading the Word daily. Everything I read fascinated me. I'd wanted to share my biblical "revelations" with my husband but he wasn't interested. I would go to church and come home elated. I'd try to share what the pastor said at that morning's service. Vernon didn't care. His attitude soon wore me down and I decided to leave him alone. I learned to pour my expectation for a better life into God's hands.

Vernon and I may have lived together, but we were worlds apart. Where I once looked to share life's experiences with Vernon, I sought out other believers because I felt they would be the only ones who could understand my spiritual transformation. I listened to Christian educational tapes and music. I went to conferences. Wherever the people of God were going to meet, I wanted to be there. To Vernon's credit he never tried to stop me from learning, but he never joined me either. The entire time that I was attempting to learn more about the Lord, I thought Vernon wasn't remotely interested. What I didn't know was that Vernon was silently watching me from a distance. He would take note of every change I made and wonder how long it was going to last. Was this a fad, or was this permanent? He never asked me anything, but he watched my every move.

Still unhappy and lonely at home, I thought maybe if I changed my behavior and acted more Christ-like, maybe I could win Vernon to the Lord. I wasn't sure what godly behavior looked like, so I began to look for examples. Big mistake!

As I began to take a closer look at the people around me, I discovered that many of them would say one thing, but do something totally different. The more I read the Word, the more I didn't see what it meant to be Christian among the people I associated with at the base. I didn't see people who loved each other unconditionally. I didn't see people who lived what they preached. The more I read, the more disgusted I became with the hypocrisy. It soon became clear that I couldn't stay "saved" in Spain. Before I knew it I had backslidden. I started hanging out with my girlfriends and partying again. I knew I was wrong. I knew God wanted something better for me, but I didn't have the strength to walk the straight and narrow in Spain.

The young man at my church who first witnessed to me grilled the importance of the rapture into my head. He showed me in the Bible where it says that one day the Lord Jesus was going to break through the clouds and those who were faithful to Him would be caught up to meet him in the air, (1 Thess. 4:17). I wanted to be one of the chosen that would be "caught up" to meet Jesus, but I knew I wasn't ready to make that kind of commitment to the Lord. So I actually prayed a real crazy payer: "Lord, if you could hold off on the rapture, I promise to give You my life when I get back to America and I won't turn away from You ever again."

The Lord is so merciful, because He honored my request. Vernon and I left Spain in 1976 and moved to California. As promised, I rededicated my life to Jesus. That meant no more parties, no more alcohol, and no more secular music. I cut everything out cold turkey. I also sought out Bible studies, Christian retreats, and mid-week services. I faithfully read my Word. I would send the kids to school then come home and open up the Word for a couple of hours or longer. When I promised God that I wanted to change, I meant what I said. But I still had doubts that God really heard my request.

As it happened, the military sent a guide over to our home to help us become more familiar with the area. Our guide happened to be an old friend we met when we were stationed in Florida in 1971. His name was Rossie and while we were in Florida the three of us had some wild times together. Seeing him again really made me doubt that God heard anything at all. When he walked into the house, I excused myself and went into my daughter's room to comb her hair.

Vernon was excited to see his old friend and immediately asked him about the area nightclubs. Rossie stammered. "Uh, man. I don't party any more. I'm into the Word."

My ears pricked up. With the hairbrush still in hand, I left LaVette and went back into the front room. I pointed my brush at Rossie. "I want to know one thing," I said, "are you serious? "Yeah." Rossie smiled. "My wife and I go to church service, read the Word, and have Bible studies in our home.""Fine, we'll be there," I said. Maybe God heard me

18

after all. I thought to myself. I was satisfied with his answer so I left the men to catch up.

When you join the military, you also join a family-oriented culture. The bonds you create with other young couples are strong simply because of the nature of military life. So if your friends partied, then you partied. In this case, if our friends went to Bible study, then that's where we went. That's how Vernon started getting into the Word.

I was serious about studying the Bible and so was Rossie. However, Vernon and Rossie's wife still had not submitted themselves to Christ, but one day Vernon surprised us. We had been studying the Word together for a few months and we were in a season when there is great turnover in the military. Several of our members were being reassigned. This particular night the Bible study was at our house. We studied as usual, and when the lesson was over Rossie always asked if any of us needed prayer. Up until this point, Vernon always said no thank you to the request. As far as he was concerned he didn't need prayer. This night, however, my husband had a change of heart.

"Yes, I want you to pray for me because I am going to ask Jesus to come into my heart tonight."

I was in shock. I cried a joyous river. I couldn't believe that my husband was surrendering his life to the Lord. For the first time in several years, hope sprang into my heart like an old friend. Even though hope found its way back into the Ashley household, it didn't change the fact that Vernon and I were still emotionally, spiritually, and mentally divorced from each other. Though we were now saved and walking with the Lord, Vernon had his Jesus and I had mine. We'd read the Word in different rooms from different Bibles. Hurt lingered in our hearts and there was no healing for our broken relationship.

A few months after Vernon's transformation, we had a

mutual friend who was in a difficult situation and we were led to pray for him — together. I found myself with Vernon at the foot of our bed on our knees praying for our friend. As we cried out and prayed together to the same God, we raised our heads simultaneously and looked at each other with new eyes. At that moment we both knew that the Lord was healing our hearts. As Vernon and I stared into each other's eyes, I realized the man looking back at me was the same one I connected with almost nine years before. He was a little older, a lot wiser, and very tired.

Vernon and I had walked too long without God in our lives. Now, with God at the center, life didn't seem to wear on us as much, and we began to live out the dream he and I once talked about. God had lifted the deadness that once stood between us. Suddenly, we were no longer afraid of our feelings for one another. I had a new respect and forgiveness for my husband, and he had the same for me. God resurrected our dead marriage, and we were joyfully alive again.

God knitted our hearts back together. He gave us a new love for one another and a new commitment. After we realized we "liked" each other again, we searched God's Word for a new direction for our marriage. We took things slow. We decided not to be romantic. Instead we went back to our roots. We worked at being friends, but this time using God's instructions found in the Word of God.

God's Plan for Marriage

At the time of our conversion, Vernon and I had been together for a total of nine years. For three of those years we were dating and for the next six years we were a married couple.

Once the Lord opened my eyes, I realize those years were our time of wandering in the wilderness without a compass, water, or the proper clothing. We were trying to be married without God's help, His Word, or His armor. We were completely lost because God is the one who has the roadmap for marriage. Without God's directions a real marriage can't last. It may be interesting for a while, but to reap all the benefits that God has placed in marriage you need Him to guide you.

Vernon and I understood that the difficulties we went through up until this point was because we were living outside God's laws. We made a concerted effort to change and invest in our marriage from God's perspective. God wanted our marriage to last but He wasn't going to help us unless we did it His way. We wanted our marriage to work, so we learned to peacefully surrender to God and follow His instructions.

The first thing we learned was that marriage originated in the heart of God. It wasn't because somewhere in time man found woman and woman found man. Marriage wasn't found in the heart or the mind of man. Adam didn't know he was lonely or incomplete. God saw the need and decided to do something about it. God looked at His first fruit and said, "It's not good for man to be alone," (Gen. 2:18).

God gave Adam a wife and his role was to love, nurture, honor, and protect her. He gave Eve a husband and her role was to be a godly helper. When I got married I thought being a good wife was running Vernon's bath water, cooking his meals, and raising our kids. I didn't know I was supposed to support, counsel, encourage, and protect my husband. Vernon knew he was supposed to provide for us, but he didn't know he was also supposed to nurture me. We were clueless about our roles in marriage and what it really cost to be married.

To discover more, we went on a fact-finding mission. We went to church and marriage conferences. We listened to Christian educational tapes and music. This change was a slow process. But it happened, step-by-step and lesson-by-lesson, over many years. This wasn't an overnight change. Once we actively invested in our marriage, the coldness between us warmed up. We worked at talking, and discovered a new laughter. Through this process we learned God wanted us to make it, but we had to want God's help. His help included certain principles that couples must follow. Those principles are:

- ❖ Leaving and cleaving
- ❖ Fighting for your marriage
- ❖ Diffusing drama
- ❖ Becoming a suitable helper
- ❖ Surrendering and submitting to one another and to God
- ❖ Intimacy as ministry

We learned that if we followed these principles our marriage would be strengthened, and we would be able to endure as a married couple in a covenant relationship.

Please understand the principles of a successful marriage did not unfold before us in a neat little package. We stumbled our way through the process — falling down and getting back up, but always determined to do things God's way.

I can remember in the very beginning of this journey when God was dealing with me about the principle of submission. God didn't send a person to teach me the principles. Instead, He delivered His message to me in a little book entitled, *"Me? Obey Him?"* This little 99-cent book was a like a hammer. It said three things that were nailed into my heart: 1. Submit to your husband. 2. Honor your husband. 3. Respect your husband.

I fell on my face after reading the last page and cried out to the Lord. "But God, you don't know him. The Lord answered and said, "I made Vernon. I know him better than you!" "If I do what the woman who wrote this book says, Vernon is going to have me doing all kinds of crazy things," I contended. "Lord, you know that a white woman wrote this book. She never had to live with a black man. They're different." I could almost hear God laughing at me. "Listen," He said, "what the author shared in her book is a result of what she got from *My* Book. It's not an issue of you submitting to him. It's an issue of you submitting to Me! When you can submit to Me, you won't fear submitting to your husband. After the Lord and I had a good talk, I surrendered to God's will for my life and from that day forward I submitted to my husband.

Chapter 3
Becoming One Flesh

Moving from my father's house to my husband's house was a clear example of the biblical principle of "leaving and cleaving." However, after digging into God's Word, I learned that this principle is much broader than moving from one house to another. In the deeper levels of *leaving and cleaving,* it is all about two people being transformed into *one flesh.* It also applies to the mental, emotional, and spiritual aspects that every couple will experience in a Christ-centered marriage relationship.

Step-by-step I learned about the process of marital transformed as I took on the task of meeting the needs of Vernon and our children. They were now my first priority and responsibility. Being married meant that I had to "leave" my dependency on Mama and Daddy in order for me to "cleave" to my husband. My father and mother could no longer be the ones who came to my rescue, because that was Vernon's role. If I had questions or concerns, my first thought would be to call my dad. But now that I was married I had to learn to go to Vernon first. He had to be my confidant and the one I depended on to help me make decisions and to meet my needs. *Leaving and cleaving* meant changing my mindset from "me and my" to "we and ours."

God designed marriage with the concept of "we-ness" in mind. Let's go back to Gen. 2:18-24. When God noticed that Adam was alone in the world, God said Adam's aloneness wasn't good. Adam needed a companion — someone to share his life and someone to be a source of mutual support. God understood that for Adam to succeed and thrive as a person, he needed a support system. He needed someone to share his dreams and share the work. He needed someone who was his equal and fully able to share the joys and pleasures of life.

During our years of marriage Vernon and I learned the secret of how God transforms us from "me" to "we." As I look back I can identify the major keys to becoming one flesh.

Cut All Soul Ties

It is important for couples to identify and separate themselves from any relationships that might hinder them from cleaving emotionally and mentally to one another. Understand that your marriage is precious. Learn to protect what God has blessed you with by being protective toward your mate. Finally, let God heal your old wounds so He can firmly knit your hearts together.

You will never become completely "one" with your mate until you cut all soul ties. A soul tie is a relationship where you are bound or joined to someone in a way that is emotionally unhealthy. Carrying a soul tie in your heart will wreak havoc in your marriage. Some of us, though married, still have soul ties to ex-husbands and ex-wives, and with ex-boyfriends and ex-girlfriends. There are many ways to develop a soul tie, but the result is always the same: a secret bondage to someone else will always keep your marital relationship out of balance.

In my marriage to Vernon, it became evident that there were soul ties that needed to be broken for Vernon and I to become "one flesh." My husband was is his mother's youngest son. As a little boy, his father would always tell Vernon he had to take care of his mother. Vernon's father was a disabled Veteran who was in and out of the hospital because of an illness he developed while in the military. Whenever his dad was in the hospital, Vernon became the "little man" of the house. He was his mother's emotional support. He was the ear his mother bent when she needed someone to listen. Because of this, Vernon and his mother shared a very tight bond, or a soul tie. It was so tight that she called Vernon her million-dollar gold piece, and would often treat him as such.

His mother was the neighborhood hairdresser when I was a teen, and often did my hair. I can remember when I was dating Vernon his mother would stop doing hair to put cornbread in the oven so it would be hot when Vernon got home from his after-school job. Vernon liked hot cornbread straight from the oven and his mother made sure he had it. She did this like clockwork and without a moment's hesitation.

The way his parents viewed his responsibility to his mother created a damaging emotional soul tie and made "leaving and cleaving" to me difficult to achieve. As Vernon's wife, there was no way I could top his mother's devotion to my husband or his devotion to her. Many of our struggles in the beginning of our marriage were rooted in the soul ties they shared. After both of us became saved, we realized the effect that my mother-in-law's relationship was having on our marriage. The Lord led Vernon to speak with his parents about the matter. God showed Vernon he occupied a place in his mother's heart that rightfully belonged to his father.

After much prayer, Vernon went to his father and asked forgiveness for taking his father's place in his mother's heart. I, of course, don't mean this in a perverted way. The emotional ties of being seen as "the one to take care of his mother" and her "million-dollar gold piece" had created an emotional tie that made "leaving and cleaving" to me quite challenging. After seeking his father's forgiveness, Vernon turned to his mother and asked her forgiveness for taking his dad's place in her heart. Then in front of me and his father, Vernon said, "Mom, I want to release you now back to your husband. I want to be your son — a son that will honor you and take care of you in your old age. But, I release you back to your husband." Healing took place between Vernon and his father and mother. To this day, my husband and his mother have a godly relationship.

I also had to break a few soul-ties with my family. My husband didn't believe in being in debt, so when we moved to Oregon, he created a budget for us to live on. "Budget" was not only a foreign concept to me, but in my mind it took the fun out of living. From the beginning Vernon kept the bills paid on time and never allowed us to overspend. He worked hard to stretch every dollar. I honored Vernon's efforts by trying not to overspend the money. However, that didn't stop me from calling my father when I wanted extra money for new clothes or to go to the hairdresser.

Whenever Vernon said "no" to my financial request I would call Daddy. He never asked me why I needed the money he would just wire me the amount I requested. As a new bride, I was clueless to the fact that it was wrong to continue to ask my father for money. In my way of thinking, I had two sources of income — my husband and my daddy. No one ever told me that once I say, "I do," I was supposed to break all financial ties to my family and live on my husband's income. The idea of my father playing the role of my financial golden calf rubbed Vernon the wrong way. He resented it with a passion because he felt disrespected. Going to Daddy for money wound Vernon's pride and his manhood. It was good for me he didn't put up with this for very long.

One day Vernon politely called my mother with me standing in the room. "Mom," he said, "if we need money, I will call you and Dad. If I don't call, please refrain from giving Patricia money."

My mother agreed to honor Vernon's request and passed the word on to my father. Vernon hung up the phone and then gave me a look that said, "Don't even think about calling your family again for money!" Once the soul ties were cut, and I learned how to cleave to Vernon as my provider.

I next had to learn how to shift all the admiration I had for my father to my husband.

27

Admire and Affirm Your Man

Let me state for the record that admiring someone who continually hurts your feelings or takes you for granted requires great spiritual maturity. When Jesus said in Mat. 5:44 *"Bless those who curse you and pray for those who spitefully use you and persecute you..."* the Lord must have had married couples in mind. The idea of showing admiration for someone who may cause you pain is a hard pill to swallow, yet Jesus would not have asked us to do something that was totally impossible. You must begin with deep prayer. It is the only way to change your point of view. How you view your husbands' actions is critical to the success or failure of your marriage. If you want to stay out of divorce court, then it is important to see your husband the way God sees him — as someone who has good intentions but makes bad choices. Allow me to give you the following advice to help you keep the right attitude toward your mate.

➢ Focus on the intent, not the actions of your mate. As newlyweds, there are some things you think are cute, like the way he eats, or the way you make that humming noise when you sleep. Even how one partner may be very neat and the other can find anything in a cluttered room. But wait a few years, and what used to be cute now gets on your nerves. You no longer see your mate with "rose-colored glasses." This is where I was with Vernon after he had come to the Lord in 1976.

I have always admired my husband for his meticulous nature. Vernon is a very orderly man. Part of this comes from his military training and part is just his natural personality. Well, when you have children, being orderly doesn't always happen. So, Vernon wanted to help strengthen his family's weakness. The idea was all well and good; however, you can't get the job done by becoming a drill sergeant. Especially when you're packing for a fun family getaway.

We're campers. We enjoy connecting with nature. Vernon would take us camping often, but there was always one catch: we had to leave the house in order. Everyone had a chore and if we did our part, the house would be spotless and the camper would be packed and ready to go. But, we never did our chores fast enough or in the order that Vernon preferred. Every time this happened, Vernon would "help" us get it together by becoming a drill sergeant. After listening to him bark orders at us for half the morning, no one — except him — was in the mood for camping once we were ready to go.

It was during these moments that Vernon's meticulous nature would rub me the wrong way. Camping could have been more enjoyable if he had just relaxed. But before I could say another negative thing, God stopped me and told me to focus on the *intent* of Vernon's actions. After thinking about it, I realized Vernon didn't want us to come home to a messy house because he knew we would be tired and not in the mood to clean anything. His intent was to have us come home to a stress-free and inviting atmosphere. Vernon's intent was good, but the action that he took didn't go over too well with the family.

➢ Forgive and love your husband unconditionally. Proverbs 10:12b says, *"...love covers all sins."* The kind of love that covers all sins can only come from the heart of God. Once we really fall in love with God, you will find that the He will cover your imperfections and allow you to love your husband unconditionally. If your husband is a godly man, know that he is not out to hurt you on purpose. Perhaps he is still learning how to handle the woman he loves without wounding her spirit.

Armed with this knowledge, learn to compliment your husband in spite of what he says or does. Call those things as not as though they were. If you say, "Honey, you are so thoughtful," he will appreciate the compliment and eventually become more thoughtful. God showed me that a compliment to a man is like water on a plant. The outcome is always the same — they blossom. Even if your husbands initially reject the compliments, or act like your words don't matter, trust me when I say not only does your husband like the compliments, but also he needs them. The best barometer of his need for appreciation and admiration is watching our children with our husbands. Children know how to adore their daddies. There is nothing our husbands won't do for their sons and especially for their daughters.

Our daughter LaVette is grown, married, and has children of her own. Yet she still has a certain amount of influence over her dad. It all began when she was about 5 years old. I often wondered why my husband would jump at her requests. So, I started watching them more closely. She would sit at the dinner table, point at what she wanted and he would get it for her. She never said a word. I'd asked myself, "What is this? I don't have that kind of influence. I'm going to watch her, and whatever she does, I'm going to do that." I didn't say this because I was jealous. No. I wanted them to have a loving, healthy relationship. I just believed Vernon's heart was big enough for the both of us. So by watching my daughter with her daddy, I learned how to treat my husband.

As he worked on the car, she'd sit by the side of the car and talk with him. So I started doing the same thing. When he'd cut the grass in the backyard, she'd walk up and down the lawn talking with him. So I started doing the same thing plus fix him a cold drink and serving it to him. When he'd come home from work, she'd happily run to the door greeting him with a great big hug. She always sweetly asked, "How are you doing, Daddy?" She acted like her day was just beginning when he walked in the door.

I watched her pull off his shoes after he settled in for the night from a long day at work. She'd always say, "Daddy, do you want me to take your shoes off?"

He'd kick back in the easy chair and say, "Yes." Then, she'd massage his feet.

I was amazed at how a little adoration would ease my husband's mind and emotions. His whole disposition would change. So taking my child's cue, I started greeting him at the door. I started taking off his shoes and massaging his feet. At first he thought I was crazy. He was even a little suspicious. But I was a woman on a mission. My daughter had taught me that love reciprocates. So I figured if it worked for her, it should work for me. After a matter of time, once I started rubbing Vernon's feet, he started taking off my shoes and rubbing my feet. With each kind act that he would show, I would praise him and tell him all the good things I loved about him. And of course, he started telling me about all the good things he loved about me. By being able to compliment one another and look at each other through God's eyes, it ultimately strengthened our relationship.

Watch Each Other's Backs

Another aspect of "leaving and cleaving" is protection. As little girls, most of us looked to positive male figures as protectors. But once we became married women, God intended for our husbands to protect us and for us to protect them.

In the beginning, God required obedience from Adam as a means of protecting him. He instructed Adam not to eat of the tree of knowledge of good and evil because he would die, (Gen. 2:17). The moment Adam and Eve rebelled in the Garden of Eden, sin entered the world. As a result, God instituted laws and systems to restore order and to protect us from the hostile environment that sin created. These laws and

31

systems are found in God's Word. In fact, King Solomon wrote a proverb telling his children the blessing of keeping God's commands. He said, *"My son, do not forget my law, but let your heart keep my commands; for length of days and long life and peace they will add to you,"* (Prov. 3:1). When we trust God and obey Him implicitly, we live. When we rebel against God's laws and ignore His counsel, we suffer the consequences.

As humanity grew in numbers and developed into communities, God anointed men and women to be watchmen for the people. The word "watchmen" or "watchman" is used 80 times in the Bible. A "watchman" means to look out, peer into the distance, spy, watch, and scope out in order to see approaching danger. It is often used in reference to the king's guards, those who look from a city tower, or God's prophets. Watchmen were given the charge to be the eyes and ears of a people. With watchmen on guard, the attacks of the enemy are not a surprise.

In marriage, husbands and wives are the watchmen for one another. When God instituted marriage, He did so with the idea that the husband would protect his wife and the wife would protect her husband. Each person would watch each other's backs and warn the other of danger. Saved or unsaved husbands fulfill this role when they warn their wives about dangerous relationships or too-good-to-be-true purchases to keep us from being ripped off by an unscrupulous person. They do it when they keep our cars in good condition and ensure our homes are safe. Husbands protect us by paying bills on time. Vernon protects me when he questions some of my decisions. He'll say, "Are you sure about this?" For me, this is a yellow or red flag warning me that maybe I haven't thought something through as thoroughly as needed.

After Vernon accepted Christ, God anointed him as prophet over our family. As a prophet, our husbands carry the burden of hearing from God and then having to implement what God wants for the family. This could include relocating to another city in the middle of a school year, changing jobs midstream, or not buying the "dream" house or car or other big-ticket item that happens to look good and is sorely needed. Or, it could be as simple as adding more devotion time to the day, or taking part in a family fast that no one in the house agrees with nor understands.

My husband was big on family fasting, especially from television. Most often the fasts would come after Vernon spent time with Lord. We had a room in our house that was only reserved for prayer and devotional time. We didn't play in it, hold casual conversations in it, or speak loudly in it. In fact, God's presence was so evident if you weren't "right," your spirit wouldn't allow you to go in there. It was if God was sitting in there waiting on us. Sometimes when my husband would emerge after spending some time with the Lord, his whole face would be bent out of shape. It was at those times that we knew he had a word for us. Vernon would say the Lord wants the family to fast from TV or we need to fast from food. He would call it cutback times.

No one enjoyed Vernon's cutback times. He would unplug the TV set and shove it in the closet for two months at a time. For the first week or so, we'd go through TV withdrawal. Afterward, the family would function like a family again. The kids would talk about their days, hopes, dreams, and ambitions with more clarity and depth. They would read more and allow their imaginations to be creative. Vernon and I would experience deeper intimate times. As a family, we would experience unspeakable joy in our time spent with the Lord. We may not have initially welcomed the "cutback times," but we were always amazed at how God used those times to strengthen us and bring us closer to one another and to Him. By Vernon fulfilling his role as prophet, God was able to teach our family how to rely on one another for strength, hope, and fun, which often came in handy because of our nomadic military lifestyle.

Husbands aren't the only "watchmen" of a family. As wives and mothers it is our job to protect our children and to give our husbands wise counsel about business decisions or investments. We watch over their relationships with associates, friends, and even family. Our husbands can't see everything that comes at the family. Sometimes, there are situations that only a woman can see.

We see the strange woman coming a mile away. Strange means to turn aside, be a stranger or foreigner, to be adulterous, to be estranged, or to be "the other woman." Proverbs 5:1-13 warns against the sexual sin of the strange woman: *"For the lips of an immoral woman drip honey, And her mouth is smoother than oil; But in the end she is bitter as wormwood, Sharp as a two-edged sword. Her feet go down to death, Her steps lay hold of hell,"*(Prov. 5:3-5). The strange woman comes anytime and anywhere our husbands are in positions of power or influence. They know how to talk to our husbands to make them feel important or special. They know how to posture themselves to be invaluable to them masked in the guise of "helping or assisting." These women know how to seduce without being overt. The above Scripture describes the strange woman as smooth. But when tasted, our husbands' good names are destroyed, their families are torn apart, and their futures are blacklisted. Throughout history, the strange woman has brought down great men. In the Bible, Solomon and Sampson both fell at the hands of the strange woman.

The godly woman who keeps herself attractive and desirable can take her post as "watchman" and keep strange woman is kept at bay. In Proverbs 31 it says, *"She (the virtuous wife) watches over the ways of her household and does not eat the bread of idleness,"* (Prov. 31:27). God designed wives to discern the covert actions of people around our families and husbands. We were created to ask poignant questions concerning people's motives that others wouldn't necessarily think to ask. Our responsibility as the watchmen is to pull our husbands' coattails when a co-worker relationship looks a tad bit too cozy. Or if a "helping" situation can be misconstrued.

For example, my husband is a trustworthy man. Anyone who knows Vernon knows he can be trusted. As a young saved couple, my husband had a female co-worker who asked him to keep her jar of coins for her. She used the loose change for the candy machine. Anytime she wanted to get candy she would go to Vernon and he would give her money from her own jar. No one knew about this arrangement. From the outside, it looked as if Vernon was giving this woman money on a daily basis for her candy fix. When Vernon told me what the woman asked him to do, I told him that the only woman he needs to give money to is his wife. Give that woman her money back and tell her to find another way to "hide" her change for safekeeping.

To Vernon, he thought he was doing the woman a favor. To me, she was setting up drama that could have put Vernon in a compromising situation at work, which could have ruined his good name.

Finally, we must be careful to protect our husband's health by providing him with nutritious meals and times for relaxation as well as see to it he goes to the doctor. A husband must also make sure that his wife is not be overworked and gets enough rest and exercise as well as ensure she sees her gynecologist.

Healing Old Wounds

Believe me when I say, that you can't cleave to your husband until you are healed of old wounds. If your mate has wounded you, then ask God to come into your heart and heal your hurts. Healing involves getting the misunderstanding or wrongdoing out in the open. It may take the help of a pastor or a counselor, but the work must be done. It is also important to understand that forgiveness is a process. Saying, "I forgive you," doesn't mean that your hurt feelings will immediately leave. What it does mean is that you have opened your heart to rebuild the trust that has been broken. For the healing to come, you will have to let go of unrealistic expectations that you wanted your husband to fulfill especially when he doesn't even know about your expectations. You must also learn to take a more sober view of what marriage is about. The hurts will come — they are part of living and growing together. Remember your marriage is about learning to love your husband according to the biblical definition of love and not the world's standard of love.

One way to help you reach a better understanding of your husbands' failures is to see your relationship through his eyes and his emotions. By doing this, it might help you to understand why he responds to you the way he does. Your husband is no more equipped to handle all of your emotional needs than you are equipped to handle his. When you come to this realization then you should be ready to ask God to answer the following prayers:

> ➤ "Lord, I don't expect him to be sensitive to me out of his own will, but I pray that You will move in my husband's heart and be sensitive to me through him.

> ➤ "Lord, I don't expect him to love me unconditionally. But I expect You to touch his heart in such a way that You can love me unconditionally through him.

> ➤ "Lord, I don't expect him to dwell with me according to knowledge, but I expect You to teach my husband how to live with me according to your Word.

Perhaps you are wondering what we can accomplish by

praying the previous prayer? First, you have placed the weight of your expectations on God and not your mate. Secondly, you no longer need to have confrontations with your husband to get what you want from him. Instead, you can confront the Lord in prayer and wait for Him to move. Third, instead of expecting your husband to be your all-in-all, you can find that fulfillment in your relationship with the Lord.

Understand that even after all of the forgiving, loving, surrendering and trusting in God — your husband may not respond to you in the way you hoped. That's OK. Don't stop trusting God. Don't stop obeying God. Know that God is quietly doing a work in your marriage. It may not look like it in the natural, but it's happening. After all, marriage is a faith walk.

"Leaving and Cleaving" Is a Choice

It took Vernon and I thirteen years to learn how to leave and cleave. By 1983, we had lived in Oregon, Florida, Spain, California, and the Netherlands. During the journey, Vernon and I had finally become one flesh. Both of us came to understand the fundamentals of what it takes to make a marriage work. We each had invested time, love, sweat, and blood into our relationship. We had devoted our lives to Christ and were willing to conduct our marriage God's way. The Lord in his grace and mercy was finally able to knit our hearts back together, so much so that when we moved back to California in 1983 we were extremely sensitive to each other's moods as well the motives of the people around us. Finally, God had us in a place where He could give us the tools that we needed to ensure that all He had done to make us "one flesh" no one could tear apart.

CHAPTER 4
Marriage Is a High-Risk Venture

I moved the last box into our new condo. It's not what Vernon wanted, but it was nice and clean and an improvement over our small row house in the Netherlands. I was so glad to be back in the States. Home at last. We moved to Highland, California in 1983. The possibilities were now endless and the idea to see my family outweighed my current simmering attitude toward my husband. Vernon and I just finished with our spat and he was giving me the silent treatment. I had learned that letting him stew until we could talk rationally saved us a lot of hurt feelings. I was trying to be the peacemaker Mama had told me about when I first got married almost 13 years before. So, I shrugged my shoulders and kept on working. As I passed our hallway mirror, I caught him watching me with a cold, disgusted stare. His look caught me off guard. I thought, "OK, girl. You pushed Vernon too far. Pull it in, and find a way to win his favor."

Winning Vernon's favor always meant fishing. Vernon loves fishing. It's his favorite pastime. But, he disliked fishing with me because I didn't know how to keep quiet. I wanted to talk. Have meaningful dialogue. Or, I would read. Either way my activities would disturb him, and he would always tell me, "Patricia, be quiet. You scare the fish away."

I didn't suggest the idea until after dinner. You can always talk to a man on a full stomach. The house was clean, the kids were in bed, and we were watching TV. I leaned over to him.

"Vernon, let's go fishing."

He looked at me very suspicious. "Why," he asked in a measured tone.

"It's been awhile. Let's go."

"…OK."

We got up at the crack of dawn the next day and loaded the van. I had to reassure Vernon that he wasn't making a mistake by agreeing to take me with him. "Vernon, I'm going to go fishing with you today, and I'm not going to take any books, and I'm not going to rush you. We can stay as long as you want, and I promise you we're going to catch fish." I also had to promise him that I wouldn't try to engage him in meaningful conversations like our last fishing attempts.

All while we drove to the lake, I prayed to God. "Lord, sanctify my mind so I can enjoy this fishing trip with my husband. Help me to have pleasure and fun. Let him enjoy me. Father in the name of Jesus you know I don't like fishing, but I love Vernon. I want this to be the best fishing trip he's ever had. Now Lord, You know where all the fish are so when Vernon throws his hook out, let the fish come over to where we are so he can catch fish and have fun today."

While we parked and sat on the bank of the water, I said to Vernon, "We're going to catch a lot of fish today. So, just to show the Lord we believe it, let's throw back the first three fish we catch."

"Oh, you've got to be crazy," he said.

But we did it anyway. It took us forever to catch the first three fish, but we threw them back. Now I prayed, "Lord, please let him catch fish. Father this is sacrificial love. This is my desire to please You and find favor with my husband. God, please let us catch fish."

After I prayed, the fish kept biting. That night we came home with a large cooler filled with fish. Vernon was so happy with me and I was excited. I remember saying to myself, "I'm getting deeper and deeper in his heart."

Prepare to Do Battle

With both of us committed to the Lord, we found ourselves pulling away from old habits and old friends, and moving toward new habits and godly friends. Making this transition was not easy. But we knew we would have to try. Sometimes we would succeed by not arguing, not giving each other the cold shoulder, or by simply apologizing first. Other times we'd fail by holding on to a friendship with people whose negative attitudes weren't conducive to our new way of life. There were times when the transition would be painful, especially when people who knew us before we were saved stopped supporting us because they didn't believe our transformation was real. In any case, we were determined to move forward regardless of others' opinions or our own shortcomings.

When we find ourselves in this phase of our relationships, or at similar crossroads, understand this is a time when we must actually fight for our marriages. Know that Satan doesn't want our marriages to succeed. His whole purpose is to seek and destroy whenever and however possible, and he will use any and everything to throw us off course.

Satan is a savvy strategist. Like a general in the military, he has studied humanity and discovered our stronghold, or power base, is the home. If Satan can destroy the home, he also destroys the Church, because the Church depends upon the strength and stability of marriages and families. If he destroys the Church, then he destroys God's ultimate plan for humanity — everlasting life in Him. The operative word here is "if". *If* Satan destroys our marriages, then he wins. So we as Christians must make sure he doesn't succeed.

How does Satan destroy marriages? He attacks the way he has always attacked — in the spaces of our hearts where

God is no longer in control. Where there is an absence from God, Satan fills the void. When we are in God's protection, He fills us with love, forgiveness, truth, humility, security, trust, courage, hope, and faith. However, when we move away from God — meaning we no longer want to live by His laws — *we* create holes, or pits of darkness, in our hearts. Satan fills those holes with misunderstanding, loneliness, depression, pride, greed, lust, lies, insecurity, suspicion, hopelessness, bitterness, indifference, and ultimately hate.

Satan used this strategy on Eve while they were in the Garden of Eden. He offered Eve wisdom, *"...you will be like God, knowing good from evil,"* (Gen. 3:5). Eve and Adam bit the bait; therefore, Satan destroyed the life God had given them in the Garden. In spite of their behavior, God offered redemption by putting enmity between Eve and Satan and between her Seed and Satan's seed. *"He shall bruise your head, and you shall bruise His heel,"* (Gen. 3:15). God's strategy was to send His only begotten Son into the world to redeem it. Because Satan believed in prophecies, he knew God was serious about saving humanity. So, Satan stepped up his attacks. Now, couples weren't good enough. He wanted the seed; he wanted the families.

Satan came after Adam and Eve and he came after their seed, Cain. Satan planted jealousy in his heart. The jealousy gave way to murder and Cain slew his brother Abel. This splintered the world's first family (Gen. 4:8). But God blessed Eve with more children. Satan tried again with Herod. This time the Christ child was definitely coming. To stop the prophecy, Satan planted murder and jealousy in Herod's heart. Herod decreed that all male children under 2 years of age be killed. But Satan's plan again didn't work. An angel of the Lord warned Joseph in a dream to hide Mary and Jesus in Egypt because Herod was seeking Jesus to destroy Him, (Matt. 2:13-15). Because of Joseph's obedience, Christ lived, died, and rose again — promising to come back.

41

Guess what? Satan is at it again. Almost half of marriages today end in divorce. Women are choosing abortions instead of bringing life into the world. Our children kill each other over money, drugs, sex, and material gain all in the name of "street respect". Our eyes and ears are bombarded with filth that undermines our moral values. Many of our neighborhoods and schools are riddled with gang warfare. Many of our homes breed violence called alcoholism, molestation, and verbal, mental, and physical abuse. With road rage on the rise, the highways have become battlegrounds. Travel has a whole new meaning in the wake of recent terrorist activity. If we deal realistically with the times we live in, then we must realize Satan is serious about destroying us.

The only way we can neutralize Satan's strategic plan is to draw closer to God and reject Satan's empty promises. Leave no room in our hearts for Satan to enter. Satan can only work in the areas of our lives where God isn't in control. Therefore, we must voluntarily bind ourselves with God because apart from Him there is no victory.

Recognize Signs of Marital Sickness

Binding ourselves to God means we must stop feigning ignorance about the devices Satan uses to attack our marriages. We must take the blinders off our eyes in order to clearly see the signs exclaiming our marriages are in trouble.

One sign is the loss of intimacy with our husbands like holding hands, sharing thoughts, or expressing emotions. Intimacy is lost when we can't look into each other's eyes, or don't feel like connecting with our husbands physically. Our body language can communicate, "come close" or "stay away". Pay attention if you've experienced or done any of the following:

❖ Move to the edge of the bed, pretend to be asleep, or read a book instead of connecting physically with your husband

❖ Refuse to share your day with one another

42

- ❖ Stop fueling one another's dreams
- ❖ Stop affirming one another
- ❖ Stop praying together
- ❖ Replace couple time with work, children, or other activities

When we do one or more of the above on a consistent basis, our marriages are potentially in trouble because the area where intimacy once filled has been depleted. Satan can use this depletion to gain entry into our hearts. He'll make the activities in our lives a wedge between our husbands and us that keeps us from strengthening and building our marriages. Here's what happens: As we draw closer to the activities of our lives, we detach ourselves from our husbands and lose our connection to God. Suddenly, we start feeling tired and overworked. This gives way to resentment because we feel as though our husbands aren't supporting our efforts in the ways in which we think they should. Then we allow our minds to wander and create scenarios that don't exist. These scenarios leave us open to becoming *justified* in being upset with them. Now Satan turns those frustrations into wedges that drain us of the joy, laughter, and fellowship we previously experienced in our marriages. Those feelings are now replaced with sorrow, anger, and estrangement. In Satan's strategy, he has used the void of intimacy to destroy our marriages.

But it doesn't have to be this way. We can fight back — take a stand. The best way to defeat Satan's attacks is to open the lines of communication with our husbands; honor and respect them; trust God; and as a couple ensure we wear the whole armor of God.

Defeat Satan's Attacks: Open Lines of Communication

Opening the lines of communication means knowing how to forgive and sometimes saying "I'm sorry" first.

Vernon and I were on our way to the airport. He didn't want us to be late for our flight, and felt I wasn't moving fast enough to make that happen. So, he raised his voice at me to get me to speed up. Instead of looking at him as if he had lost his mind or pick a fight, I shut my mouth and picked up my pace. Deep in my heart I knew we had plenty of time, and at the rate we were going, we would be extra early. But, I said nothing. I was trying to be that peacemaker Mama told me about years before. After checking in, I looked at my watch, and sure enough, we had more than enough time. Boiling inside, I wanted Vernon to apologize for the way he had spoken to me. But he just moved on as if everything was normal. The Lord pricked my heart. He told me to apologize first, so I did. I turned to Vernon and apologized for being insensitive to his effort to get us to the airport on time. He smiled at me, and forgave me. Then he asked for my forgiveness for the way he had spoken to me, and I forgave him. He took my hand and we moved to the waiting area, putting the whole incident behind us so we could enjoy the trip.

Scripture calls the ability to forgive and ask for forgiveness a sign of being a peacemaker. In Matthew 5:9, Jesus told the disciples *"Blessed are the peacemakers, for they shall be called sons of God."* God is the supreme Peacemaker and to be a son or daughter of God means to follow His example. Being a peacemaker is a mighty tool to break Satan's hold on our marriages. When we forgive, we open the floodgates for understanding. To understand literally means to *stand under* someone else's point of view. Forgiveness allows us to see the situation from God's perspective and ultimately from our husbands'. I believe if I had not said, "I'm sorry" first, our vacation may have been ruined. I would have allowed resentment and anger to rule my heart the entire time we were together. Instead, forgiveness allowed us to clean the air and start over with a new understanding.

Communicating with our husbands also means we learn to guard our tongues. In Proverbs 21:23, it says *"Whoever guards his mouth and tongue keeps his soul from troubles."*

This is so true. Often, we can avoid many of the problems we face if we choose to respond to obstacles with love and kindness as opposed to heated debates, fiery accusations, and/or false assumptions.

When God showed me I had the power of life and death in my tongue, I began to watch what I said and how I said it. Not sugarcoating my feelings, but speaking with my husband in a way that would allow him to hear me without him feeling disrespected. Essentially, I learned to speak to my husband in love and in truth.

Defeat Satan's Attacks: Honor and Respect Your Husband

It was at this point that God challenged me to honor and respect my husband. In 1 Timothy 1:17 it says, *"Now unto the King eternal, immortal, invisible, the only wise God be honor and glory forever and ever. Amen."* God would have us honor the Lord Jesus. He would have us lift Him up, adore Him, and worship Him. As an example of that, God would have us honor our husbands.

For many of us, God had nothing to do with our choice in husbands. Instead of waiting for God's man, we got our man and ended up with Freddy Krueger. Now I have never seen the Freddy Kruger movies, but when my son described the character to me, it was a good description of what we get. He said Freddy Krueger is a monster, but he doesn't appear to be a monster in the beginning. He appears to be someone you can embrace and love. Then, as soon as you do so, he turns into a monster. Does that sound familiar? When we make our own choices in mates, we end up with someone who often hurts and disappoints us.

For example, did you know there are really six people at the altar when a couple makes their wedding vows? They are:

➤ The woman she thinks she is

45

- The woman he thinks she is
- The woman she really is
- The man he thinks he is
- The man she thinks he is
- The man he really is

Only *after* the wedding vows have been said are the people who took them *really* revealed.

When we walk down the aisle and make our covenant with God, our choice then becomes God's choice. Fortunately, God knows how to transform our Freddy Kruegers into godly men. But it takes time, patience, and prayer. The Bible says a godly woman wins her husband not by her words, but by her holy and chaste conduct, (1 Peter 3:1). Therefore,

❖ We are to submit to God by honoring our husbands and loving them, even if they aren't lovable and we feel they don't deserve it.

❖ We are to submit to the will of God and honor the Word of God.

❖ We are to line up with the instructions God has given us as godly wives.

God will put pressure on our husbands to line them up with His will for their lives and the lives of our families. However, God will not work until we, the wives, get out of His way.

One day, I felt like I was at the end of myself and I fell on my face, "God, I'm sick of him. I'm tired of trying to do things right. I'm worn out. Lord, I'm not doing anything else. I'm at the end of my rope. If he's going to be fixed, You are going to have to do it."

I could sense in my spirit that God was saying, "Whew! Finally! She's going to let Me do what only I can do."

Suddenly, I felt this load ease up off of me. My back felt straighter and my heart wasn't as heavy. I felt renewed. I remember saying to myself, "Now that I don't have to work on him and fix him up, I have time and energy to begin to focus on me."

Before I could go a step further, God whispered in my heart, "The first thing I want you to do is to honor him."

"Lord, I just don't know if I can honor him."

"Honor him," the Lord insisted.

"OK, Lord."

It became very clear to me what it mean to honor my husband. One day my friend P. Bunny Wilson, challenged me to think of a man I really admired — someone other than my husband. In a healthy and godly way, I choose an elder in the church. He was a spiritual father, mature in the Lord, full of wisdom, fervent in prayer, and highly respected in the community. When I got him in the forefront of my mind, I felt humbled. Then Bunny asked, "Do you talk to Vernon like you would like to talk to him?"

I was speechless because I realized that I didn't.

The Lord showed me it's not easy to honor, admire, and respect my husband unconditionally. But this is the way God wants us to treat our husbands. He wants us to esteem them because of their position and not their disposition. God wants us to esteem our husbands because of the place God has given them and not for the way they carry out their roles.

I wasn't sold on that idea. So, I waited for God to give me other reasons for honoring my husband. But none came. Instead God said, "Honor him because of the position I have given him. Respect and submit to the position I've given him."

God didn't prick me to put His request in action that day. He waited for a moment when my daughter would be challenged to honor her father. My husband often would give the children a laundry list of chores that must be done on Saturday before he got home from work at 4 o'clock in the afternoon. This particular Saturday, the list was extra grueling. LaVette, who was in the ninth grade at the time, wailed. It was too much. She felt overwhelmed and completely discouraged. I knew it was too much, but I also knew it was more important for her to honor her dad and obey.

My response to her was critical because it would set the pace for how she would react the next time he asked her to do something that she felt was too much. So instead of agreeing with her that the list was a bit over the top, I told her to just try. I explained that God was watching our response and she needed to do this to please God. With the right attitude and a little prayer, who knows, she might be able to do the seemingly impossible.

"LaVette let's pray first and ask God to give you supernatural ability to get this job done."

I encouraged her to sing praise songs as she worked because it would lift her spirits and give her the right attitude to make this possible. All along the way, I encouraged her to continue. By the time she finished, she had a few hours to spare and was able to greet her father with a sweet attitude when he came home.

The following Saturday she attended a speaking engagement with me. On our way back, we stopped at our favorite clothing store and caught a super sale. You know one of those sales that have markdowns on the markdowns? Anyway, we were able to get twice the amount of nice things for her for the new school year. As we rejoiced over our finds, the Holy Spirit said, "Let LaVette know this was no coincidence. It was His way of blessing her obedience to her dad and also because she did it with the right spirit."

I told her. Not only did she please her father, but she also pleased her heavenly Father, who rewarded her for her obedience and faithfulness.

Just as I showed LaVette that honoring her dad was the right thing to do by insisting she try to fulfill her father's desire to do the chores, we as wives must consistently follow that example for ourselves. In fact, I still use the qualities of the elder in the church to measure how I respond to Vernon. I want to always make sure that I am honoring my husband, regardless of how I feel or what he has done.

You can also show respect by learning to take an interest in the things he likes. If your husband loves football games, then on Monday night put the kids to bed early. Put on a nice outfit. Men are turned on by what they see. You're not competing with the game. You just want him to have the best of both worlds. Make microwave popcorn. He's going to know this will be the best game he's ever watched. Put on some real nice perfume. Then, don't distract him, just sit there and watch the game. Don't ask questions at the wrong time because you want him to enjoy the game. You want it to be a good experience. During half time give him a massage.

Some of us become archenemies to our husbands on Monday nights. You can't tolerate the games or his other favorite pastimes. You don't enjoy them because you've allowed the enemy to cause your husband's pastimes to become a weapon of war between you and him. But if you want to find favor with your husband, love the things he loves. Let him know you find pleasure in knowing he is being refreshed.

This attitude works both ways. Vernon knows how much I enjoy fellowship with godly women. When I have the opportunity to do so, he expresses delight because he knows that when I am refreshed, he benefits, too.

The other half of honor is respect. If given a choice, men would rather have our respect and honor than our affection. As women, we are the ones who need love, affection, and attention, but they need to be honored and respected. If we're going to encourage, edify, and build them up, then we must respect them. To respect them, we must show them we have a servant's heart.

In the south, women know not only how to prepare the food, but how to fix the plate. My mother saw to it that no one ate until after my father blessed the food and she fixed his plate. We had to wait. Her actions demonstrated honor and respect. I'm not saying to do that unless it's something that would communicate respect to your husbands. We're living in a time when each of us must discover what it is that communicates respect to our husbands. It could be as simple as asking him questions about his job, or working with him on his favorite hobby. Whatever the interests, encourage, edify, and build him up in those areas.

Showing respect for my husband is to cook his favorite dish — beans.

One day, I was before the Lord having a good quiet time with Him and His presence was so great I could sense Him in the room. I embraced the experience and said, "Oh God, I love You so much. God, what is it that You want me to do? Whatever You say, Lord, I'll do that."

"Get up and cook Vernon his favorite pot of beans."

I sat straight up in my chair. "Satan, in the name of Jesus, I rebuke this spirit of distraction," I declared. "Surely this isn't the Lord. God wouldn't have me interrupt my quiet time with Him to get up and cook Vernon a pot of beans?!"

Let me state for the record, I don't like to eat beans much less cook them. It takes too long and you have to stand over the stove pampering and stirring them. I get tired half way through. But Vernon likes them. He especially likes them real creamy with the right kind of juice. Just thinking about the whole cooking ordeal made me tired.

I tried to dismiss the thought and get back to my time with the Lord, but He stopped talking. The joyous experience I had with Him had flattened. The thought of cooking Vernon a pot of beans ran across my mind again. So, I thought why not? God's not talking.

I washed the dry beans I found in the back of my cupboard. I put the meat on to season the beans. As I stood over my sink, the Spirit of God ministered to me. It was as if heaven literally opened up. God ministered to my heart. Through the experience God revealed to me how important it was for me to be a helper to Vernon and please him. It amazed me to know that God was so in tune and so interested in the practical experiences of my marriage. As I cooked those beans, I communed with the Lord right there at my sink.

Soon, Vernon walked in. Seeing me cook beans raised his eyebrows. Vernon knows how much I hate cooking beans. So the first thing he thought was I had wrecked the car, or the kids had gotten into trouble and I was trying to smooth things over by cooking his favorite dish. I reassured Vernon that nothing was wrecked and the kids were fine. He asked me why, then, was I cooking beans. I told him because the Lord asked me to.

"He asked you to?"

"Yeah."

Humph. Vernon stood in the kitchen looking at me and smelling the aroma of the beans. He stayed there for a few moments then left. By dinnertime, the whole atmosphere of the house had changed. We laughed, shared our day, and when the meal was finished, Vernon asked one of the kids to get the Bible. He led us in Scripture then we prayed. Watching Vernon opened up my heart. I had missed our family devotion time. For months I wanted to suggest that Vernon lead us in spending some time in the Word, but I wasn't going to ask. I wanted Vernon to suggest the activity without my input.

God whispered to me that my obedience to cook the beans changed the atmosphere of my house, which allowed the family to reach a new level of intimacy. This is what God wanted to do for us. He wanted us to spend more time with Him. I was completely floored. Who would have thought a little pot of beans could have initiated such a change in my family? It made me realize that sometimes the things we're trying to settle on our knees can be settled on the stove.

By cooking Vernon his favorite dish, I pleased my husband and changed the atmosphere in my home to one that brought glory to God. In essence, I had submitted myself to the Lord's wish to cook the beans. When we submit and obey the

Lord, we honor our husbands and essentially trust that God can work any situation out for our good and His glory. Submission is an act of trusting the Lord.

Defeat Satan's Attacks: Trust God

To help us trust God we can pray, "Lord, I just want to obey You. Though I don't understand all that is required of me, I pray You will give me clear instructions on how to honor and respect my husband. I pray You will teach me how to submit to him as the Church submits to Christ. Father please teach me the difference between manipulation and real submission. Teach me the difference between honor and flattery. Teach me Lord."

When we approach the Lord this way, we're coming to Him with a real attitude of wanting to be women of God who please Him and want to live His way. As we do this, God honors our request and guides us.

Sometimes the situations surrounding our need to submit to our husbands look odd. It is at those times we're not trusting God because we haven't spoken with Him about the situation at hand. We need to stop and pray. "God, as I cooperate with my husband and respond to him as a wise woman, I trust You're going to work this out for our good and Your glory."

There have been times when Vernon has made decisions that I felt were the wrong ones to make. I had given him counsel ahead of time, but he didn't take it. After many heartaches and headaches, I soon learned how to release those situations into God's hands and trust Him. In doing so, I learned how to submit and trust my husband. Many times I have prayed: "God, by the power of Your Spirit, I'm trusting You and I'm going to cooperate with him even though I know this is going to be a mess. Yet, I trust You. I trust You to work it out." Praying this way taught me not only to trust God, but to ask God to give my husband ears that would hear His voice, and a heart that would seek after His wisdom.

52

My husband isn't the only one who makes interesting decisions. My daughter LaVette is now married with three children and lives with her husband in Alaska. One summer they came to visit us. She had her heart set on a particular van that was her dream car. She had gone to a dealer to test drive it, and everyone she spoke with who owned the van said they enjoyed the vehicle. One afternoon Vernon came in from running errands and told LaVette he found her dream car. It was the exact color she wanted and was $10,000 below Blue Book price. LaVette just knew God was working on her behalf to make this dream come true. All she needed was her husband's OK. She was all excited when she showed him the vehicle. He took one look and told her that she couldn't buy it. LaVette was crushed. She knew they needed the van because their family had outgrown the cars they owned. But to my daughter's credit, she didn't pitch a fit or raise her voice because of her disappointment. She calmly said, "OK, baby," and left things alone. When they got back to Alaska, they discovered that LaVette's "dream car" was not practical for Alaska's harsh climate. Neither LaVette nor her husband knew this when they saw the car in California. Instead, she found another van that was more suitable for Alaska's winters. The added blessing was they were able to pay cash for it. Now they have a roomy van that is perfect for the weather and their growing family.

In this scenario, my son-in-law's "no" protected LaVette from making a poor financial choice. Sometimes as wives we don't know what God is doing in a particular situation. We just have to trust Him and trust that our husbands are hearing from Him. When I said that sometimes we must go along with poor choices, I wasn't referring to choices that would endanger the family or cause our husbands to do something illegal. Those are times when it is imperative we speak up and speak loudly. Though God may use our husbands to steer the family with bold vision and direction, God uses us as wives to be strong helpmates. We are helpers who can influence our husbands to slow down and think before taking action.

Not only do we pray that God will work out the situation, but we also pray against Satan's attacks as the situation is being worked out. We pray against Satan's desire to destroy and create havoc in our homes. God will bring the right thing to pass even when we set out on the wrong course. God turns things around when we submit and do not override our husbands.

Defeat Satan's Attacks: Put on the Whole Armor of God

Warring with Satan is a spiritual battle that can only be waged when couples are dressed with the proper armor. The Word says we are to put on the *"whole armor of God, that you may be able to stand against the wiles of the devil," (Eph. 6:10).* The armor of God includes: the girdle of truth, the breastplate of righteousness, the shoes of peace, the shield of faith, the helmet of salvation, and the sword of the Spirit as the Word of God. Once we are dressed, then we must fight for our marriages. This means we keep the lines of communication open with our husbands, honor and respect them, and trust God. By choosing to do these things we are putting Satan on notice that our families and our marriages are not to be torn asunder. We are making it clear to Satan that to get to us he has to get through God first.

If we want to save our marriages and beat the current odds, we must decide right here and right now to walk in the Spirit no matter what. Our weapons against Satan's attack are the blood of Christ, the Word, our position in Christ, and our willingness to walk in it. Effectively wielding these tools protects your marriage and ultimately defeats the enemy.

But what happens when the enemy has your face? What happens when you realize that though many of your old wounds have healed and you've learned to effectively use principles one through three, you still find yourself slipping into old habits and old arguments? When you reach this crossroad understand that the fight has changed. Your fight is now not with outside forces, but with your old nature. Understand Satan will use whatever bombs are at his disposal to destroy your marriage. Even if those bombs happen to be within you.

Once Vernon and I understood how to fight, we next had to surrender to God the last vestiges of our old natures and kick drama to the curb.

No More Drama
Chapter 5

Years ago Vernon and I had a friend that I never understood. Even though it's in the past, I don't think it's fair to give you his real name, so I'll refer to him as "Bill." This young man had a very unpleasant habit of calling his wife "that chick." He was a good guy at heart but he had some twisted views when it came to women.

Vernon was too kind-hearted to walk away from his friendship with Bill, but I would often listen to their conversations and cringe. This was Vernon's fishing buddy. In fact, during our stay in the military, Bill was one of the few friends that we stayed in touch with as we moved from one country to the next. Friends in the military are like gold — you treasure them.

But I have to tell you I had my doubts about Bill. I appreciated his friendship with Vernon because when they went fishing together my husband would always came back relaxed and refreshed. However, Vernon also came back with a "chick" attitude that included impatience, rudeness, and being thoughtless.

Normally, Vernon treats me like gold. When I say that my husband is precious, I'm not exaggerating. He will cook for me, clean my car and keep the oil changed, fix whatever needs to be fixed around the house, play with the kids, pray with me, and be tender when situations call for it. Vernon knows how to treat a woman with respect and honor. This is what I had grown accustomed to as our marriage blossomed. But whenever Vernon went fishing with Bill, he could come home with "that chick" mentality. It would permeate his language, views, and attitude. At first, I thought it was a one-time thing. So I didn't say anything. But as Vernon continued his friendship with Bill, I realized it was becoming a habit. Vernon would leave the house a respectful, loving, husband and friend. When he came back it was just the opposite. One day he came back from fishing and called me a chick. I pulled him to the side to get his attention. After I shared my feeling he apologized and explained that he had no idea that his attitude was hurting my feelings and making me uncomfortable. He didn't realize that spending time with Bill he was picking up his habit of being disrespectful to women. Thank God that when Vernon recognized the problem, he immediately decided that, when it came to his friendship with Bill, there would be no more drama.

The War Between The Old Nature and The New Nature

Drama is a result of our dueling natures. When you come to Christ, the Word says that our old natures died in Christ and that we are to live anew in Him. We can define our "old nature," as anything that the flesh desires. Our "new nature" is reflective of what our spirit desires. According to Galatians 5:17-21, our flesh desires adultery, fornication, uncleanness, lewdness, idolatry, sorcery, hatred, contentions, jealousies, outbursts of wrath, selfish ambitions, dissentions, heresies, envy, murder, drunkenness, and revelries. Gal. 5:22-23 states that our spirit desires love, joy, peace, longsuffering, kindness, goodness, faithfulness, gentleness, and self-control. When you live in the spirit, your lifestyle reflects the desires of the spirit. When you live in the flesh, your life reflects what the flesh wants. The challenge is to be able to continue to walk in the spirit even with people who don't necessarily walk in the Spirit nor do they want too walk in the Spirit.

Walking in the Spirit takes a conscious effort on your part, because it means keeping your attitude and motives in check at all times. Let's revisit Vernon and his fishing buddy, Bill. Vernon and I had done quite a bit of work rebuilding our relationship changing the attitudes that used to keep us at each other's throats. What we didn't realize is that sometimes, even when the work had been done, temptations continue to knock on your doors trying to encourage the old nature to resurface. In this case, Vernon's fishing buddy inadvertently brought out traits of "insensitivity" in my husband. When Vernon's old nature resurfaced, my old nature of "defiance" crept in. Before we knew it, Vernon and I were arguing and allowing drama to creep back into our marriage.

The word "drama" is not used in the Bible. Instead, the word "discord" is used. Discord means to clash; or to be in a conflict that produces a clash of ideas, interests, open warfare, arguments, heated debates, or quarrels; and finally to be in strife, or angry contention to the point of rivalry. When there is drama in our homes, or when there is drama in our lives, know that chaos and disorder reign.

To nip drama in the bud, we have to set our minds on the things of the Spirit. *"For to be carnally minded is death, but to be spiritually minded is life and peace," (Rom. 8:6).* Setting our minds on the things of the Spirit sometimes proves challenging because it means cutting ties with people whose attitudes are contrary to the Spirit. This can sometimes include family members and old friends.

Vernon and I decided that in order to ensure that our old natures would not have an opportunity to resurface we would have to be careful about of people we associated with. We also made it a point to become a source of godly influence on our circle of friends and not be influenced by some of their negative ways. Drama kills — if you allow it to rule your marriage. Drama has to be cut down at the root. There is no compromise with drama. It either dies or it rules your life forever.

The Root of Drama

Drama originated in the Garden of Eden with Adam

and Eve's decision to disobey God and eat of the forbidden fruit, (Gen. 3). God commanded Adam and Eve not eat of this fruit of the tree of knowledge. That was God's one specific no-no. All Adam and Eve had to do was remember what God said and *obey*. However, operating under the influence of Satan, they chose to pursue knowledge. The scripture reminds us of the following: *"There is a way that seems right to a man, but its end is the way of death," (Prov. 14:12).*

The decision that Adam and Eve made quickly introduced them to a lifestyle ruled by drama. God then told Eve she would give birth in sorrow and pain and her desire will be for her husband who may rule over her. God told Adam because he heeded his wife's voice over God's command, thus abdicating his role as leader; the ground would be cursed and Adam would have to toil for his food until he died (Gen. 3:1-19).

Because of their actions, Adam and Eve were also kicked out of the Garden, and rebellion entered the world. Rebellion is the root cause of drama. Rebellion leads to confusion and shame, and that is why Adam and Eve hid from God when He called for them in the Garden (Gen. 3:9-10).

Shame disconnects us from God because it makes us hide ourselves. We don't like showing our faces when we've sinned or we are ashamed of something we did. By hiding, we also lose our peace and a sense of our self-worth. This spells disaster in any marriage relationship. When one partner has a rebellious nature, they challenged all authority. This desire violates the purpose of love and the marriage covenant.

Rebellion will cause a husband or wife to promise that they will change their behavior, but they will never keep their word. Rebellion will cause a husband or wife to violate the boundaries that they have established for the well being of the marriage. Rebellion totally undermines the trust a husband and a wife have in one another. When the husband fails to be the spiritual leader, his wife feels insecure. When a wife fails to submit to her husband's authority, he feels ineffective.

The following types of rebellion practiced by a husband can result in major marital drama:

- ❖ When a husband does not discipline his children of support his wife in her attempt to discipline the children.
- ❖ When a husband ignores his wife and praises and admires other women.
- ❖ When a husband shows affection to his wife only when he wants to sexual intimacy or some other favor.
- ❖ When a husband spends money without considering the needs of his wife and family.
- ❖ When a husband shows resentment when his wife achieves her personal or professional goals.
- ❖ When a husband refuses to talk to his wife about his feelings and refuses to listen when she verbalizes her needs.
- ❖ When a husband refuses to listen to his wife's advice, but will listen to friends or co-workers.
- ❖ When a husband makes major decisions without consulting his wife. When a husband neglects domestic needs around the house, like home repairs and household clean-ups.
- ❖ When a husband stays away from the home without his wife knowing where he is or when he will be returning.
- ❖ When a husband refuses to be involved in any type of spiritual activities. This includes prayer, church attendance, or reading the Bible.

A rebellious wife can be just as bad as rebellious husband. She can damage and even destroy her marriage with the following acts of rebellion.

- ❖ She refuses to submit to her husband's authority or take his advice.
- ❖ She disrespects him in front of family, children and friends.

* She refuses to make the children submit to his authority.
* She is never satisfied with what her husband provides for her.
* She gives more attention to her work or friends than she does to her husband.
* She rejects his spiritual leadership and authority in the home.
* She argues with her husband and will never admit that she is wrong or apologize about anything.
* She openly compares her husband to other men and their accomplishments.
* She makes major decisions without his input or approval.
* She uses sexual intimacy as a tool to get what she wants from him.

Whenever one or both partners in a marriage are rebellious the family experiences utter chaos, disorder and drama. When a family is in the throws of drama, peace has no place in their relationship or home. This chaotic state always begins and with disobedience to God's plan for the family.

Harmony Neutralizes Drama

Remember the principle of leaving and cleaving? Here is where the application of this principle becomes critical. When man and wife cleave to one another they "become one flesh." Becoming one flesh speaks of the harmony God wants couples to experience in a fulfilled marriage. This oneness of becoming *"bone of my bones and flesh of my flesh"* as described in detail in Genesis 2:23. Living in harmony and becoming one is reiterated in Ephesians 5:25, *"Husbands, love your wives as Christ loved and sacrificed His life for the church and gave Himself for her."* Proverbs 5:18 says, *"Let your fountain be blessed, and rejoice with the wife of your youth."*

These scriptures point to the fact that *drama* was not a part of God's plan for marriage. In fact, it wasn't in His plan for all of humankind. God has always wanted us to live in total harmony with Him and with one another. In many translations of the Bible the word "agreement" is used in place of "harmony." To be in *agreement* means to be on one accord. It also means to be joined together in the soul; to be co-spirited; likeminded, in unity and in cooperation with one another. To be in *agreement* denotes a certain level of companionship. God wanted to create a being with His likeness, His spirit, and a free will. With free will, God's divine intention was that we choose to love and obey God without the use of any laws, force or threats. God and humanity would be companions. In God's mind and in God's heart, harmony was to be fourfold:

❖ Communion
❖ Completion
❖ Fellowship
❖ Purpose

Harmony was in place before the beginning of time. Before God created man and before God created the earth, there was eternity, and in it there was total and complete harmony. Everything operated in a peaceful, divine plan and purpose according to God's will. Everything that God created lived in harmony with God, and all other creations. Peace reigned, and we experienced a fulfilling relationship with God as His companion in the Garden of Eden. In Gen. 3:8 it says that the Lord God walked in the Garden at the cool of the day calling out to Adam. God dwelled with Adam and Eve. His relationship with humanity was so intimate that Adam knew God's voice and His very presence. God's face was not hidden from Adam. God was not a stranger to humanity, and humanity was not a stranger to God. The two knew each other very well.

We have no clue as to how much time passed in which God, Adam, and Eve spent in perfect communion with one another. The Bible doesn't say but what is evident is that the intimate relationship that God created with humankind, He also nurtured.

Sin and rebellion severed this harmonious relationship. Jesus' death brought God and humanity back together again. Jesus' shed blood repaired our fellowship and companionship with God. Because of Jesus' sacrifice we can now experience harmony in the following ways:

- ❖ Harmony with God (communion) — Because of the blood of Jesus we can now enjoy an intimate relationship with God.
- ❖ Harmony with ourselves (completion) — when we experience God's forgiveness, we are free of guilt and shame. Then we can live in the fullness of who we are and why we were created.
- ❖ Harmony with others (fellowship) — we can only give to others what we are experiencing with God.
- ❖ Harmony with the earth (purpose) — As a result of being in fellowship with God and at peace with ourselves, we are then able to understand our mission here on earth.

To have this harmony, we must walk in obedience to God. We will experience harmony and peace to the same degree that we obey God's law. We will experience disharmony and loss of peace, to the same degree that we disobey God's law.

This is why divorce is so damaging. Divorce severs God's divine plan for couples to work through their differences and ultimately experience marital harmony. Divorce is *the way that seems right to us* when a marriage is falling apart. When couples experience arguments and hurt feelings on a daily basis rather than the joy and peace God intended for them to have, then divorce seems to be the only way to end the suffering. Divorce happens when pride and self-centeredness take control of the marriage and God is not in the picture.

Marriage should be as strong as a three-strand cord consisting of the husband, the wife, and God. However, when you force God out of your marriage, it becomes like a runaway train heading for a brick wall. Communication shuts down and emotional or sexual adultery can happen at any time or place. This is, of course what fuels the runaway train and makes for unbelievable drama. Once you hit the wall and break into pieces the family, as you knew it quickly disintegrates. In the aftermath, many broken people erect walls around our hearts to protect themselves from experiencing more pain. To make matters worse, they completely shut God out of our lives. Divorce completely destroys harmony.

Godly Wives and Godly Husbands

Marriages don't have to end in divorce. Often, marriages end in divorce because the couple never understood their individual roles in the marriage. God's harmony for couples is rooted in the roles He created for each partner to fulfill.

God established the husband as the head of the family. This meant that God created Adam to be the co-ruler of the earth who led, protected, and tended to the living things as well as to the earth itself. He was also created to be the one whom God spoke with to give a vision for the earth and the family.

As leader, Adam's job was to tend and keep the garden, (Gen. 2:15). The word "tend" means to cultivate, take care of, and watch over. God's intention was that Adam be made a steward over the Garden — someone trustworthy to watch and cultivate that which God had made. God also gave Adam instructions on how he should conduct himself in the Garden. God meant for Adam to share these instructions with Eve, who would become co-laborer with Adam in the Garden as well as co-ruler of the earth. As leader, it would be Adam's job to insure that Eve be privy to all information concerning the Garden and the earth. The last instructions given to Adam were to name every living thing — including woman/Eve.

After naming every living thing, Adam was given the task of protecting all living creatures that dwelled within the Garden. As protector, Adam was to guard and shield the animals and Eve from danger. He was to defend the territory that God had given them. Part of defending the territory was obeying God in all things. Adam's obedience to God acted as a shield around the Garden. As long as Adam was in right relationship with God, all was well.

The last thing Adam was to be was a prophet, or visionary and creative thinker for all living creatures in the Garden. As prophet, Adam was responsible for hearing God's voice and telling Eve what He said. Although Eve had her own relationship with God, He still spoke to Adam only about certain issues because Adam was created the head of the family.

After creating Adam and seeing there was not a suitable helper among all the living things that he named, God created woman as a helpmate for the man. Her role is to aid, assist, and minister to her husband. A helper is not an inferior person. Doctors and lawyers are our helpers. They are able to care for us in ways that we can't care for ourselves. It is no different with a wife being a "helper." In the Hebrew language, the word for "helper" is *"ezer."* This is her God-given role. If as a wife you are not an *"ezer"* to your husband, then you are inviting drama into your marriage.

As an aid to Adam, Eve's job was to help Adam fulfill the vision for the family. Her assignment was to aid, assist, and minister to Adam so the vision would become a reality. In order for Adam to be the leader of the family, the Lords ordained that the wife would be in submission to her husband, even as her husband was called to be in submission to God.

The prefix of the word submission is sub — meaning to get under. This is a *voluntary* position. When we submit, we are saying we willingly set aside our desires for the good of the family and for the good of the vision. This only works if the wife has a relationship with God. In that relationship, the wife's heart is tender toward the desires God has for her. She willingly obeys God in all things — including helping her husband by being in submission to him.

By submitting to your husband, you are getting under, or supporting their mission/vision for the family. You are called to work with them to bring the vision to fruition. Getting rid of drama begins with following your husbands' leadership. However, if you have no relationship with God and your heart does not desire to please God, you will never submit to God's family order. You will never be able to submit to your husband because you cannot submit to God first. The opposite of submission is resistance. So, instead of submitting to your husband, you will resist your husbands plan with the use of manipulation or open rebellion. With the use of either of these tools you can completely destroy the vision the God has for your family by taking over your husband's position as leader of the home. This always leads to chaos and drama.

Proverbs 14:1 it says, *"The wise woman builds her house, but the foolish pulls it down with her own hands."* You build your home by supporting your husbands' efforts. By the same toke you can tear down your home by resisting your husbands' leadership and tearing him down with your words. I learned a long time ago there is life and death in my tongue and it is up to me to choose to speak words of life or words of death. To experience true harmony in my home, I choose words of life. In choosing life, I chose to commit myself to aiding, assisting, and ministering to my husband. The more I fulfill my role, the more I experienced harmony in my home.

Wise Women Promote Harmony at Home

If you want to experience real harmony in your home — learn to set an atmosphere of peace. I gave counsel once to a young lady who has three children and is a stay-at-home mom.

A few years ago, I told her that her house should be clean and neat when her husband comes home, regardless of how much time she spends with the children during the day. I said the following words to her: "You need to make sure the house is orderly when he comes in from work. You don't need to be on the phone with your girlfriends or in front of the computer. You need to be able to receive your husband and treat him like the king of your home."

Our husbands are the kings of our families. As wives, we need to learn how to receive our kings when they come home from work. I can hear some of you now complaining that your husband doesn't act like a king. Here's the secret to changing that. Treat him as if he was already acting like the royalty God created him to be. If you continue to treat your husband like a king eventually he will start acting like one. If you raise the bar of expectation in your homes, a man will eventually rise to the occasion. If your husband often comes home with a bad attitude, or treats you with indifference when he walks in the door, or comes home when he feels like it, there are two things that are guaranteed to change his behavior: Prayer and the smell of his favorite foods cooking in the kitchen.

If you're a stay-at-home mom, clean up the house and the children before he arrives. Men love coming home to a clean house, clean children and a clean wife whose hair is neatly combed and she's wearing a nice fragrance. If you are a working wife, use the weekends to prepare your meals for the week. Place them in the freezer, or plastic bowls and then add a fresh salad or vegetable before serving. This way you won't have to come home tired from work and fix a big meal each night. A good husband who sees you working hard to prepare meals ahead of time should be more than willing to help you will the kids and the clean-up. Be sure to have a date night with your husband. This is an evening where the kids go to bed early and you plan a special evening of candles, a special meal and maybe a warm bath together. Whether you are a working woman or a homemaker make sure that you plan your days in such a way that you will not constantly be too tired for sexual intimacy.

Setting the atmosphere of our homes is so important. So often the demand of careers drains your life. When you come home you should work together to make it a restful haven. When you first walk in the door, take a few minutes for yourself, before you begin to deal with the children. When he walks in the door, allow him to have the same privilege. Make your home a place where your husband can be admired and praised and welcomed. It's our job as their wives to create such a drama-free environment.

As a good wife, do your part to promote unity within your home. Make sure that you are alert to any chaos or disharmony that will disrupt the flow of your household. If you are a wise woman, you will use discernment to gain clarity as to the root of the problems. A consistent prayer life will help sharpen your discernment. Once you discover what the problem is, use your godly influence to be a peacemaker in the family. Sometimes that may mean dying to your self-interest and pride but it's worth it, especially if it means that you are keeping drama away.

Setting the atmosphere in your home means getting up very early or staying up late at night in order to seek the Lord. It means reading your Bible and walking through the house when everyone is asleep crying out to the Lord in prayer. By doing this, you evict chaos and contention from your home.

Whenever chaos and contention would try to get the best of my family, I would get up early and play melodious praise and worship music. Then I would pray throughout the house. When the family finally woke up, the house would be completely peaceful. Whatever plans Satan had for that morning would be thwarted.

I also set the atmosphere by teaching my children how

to be friends with one another. As a military family, we were often uprooted and relocated to the next assignment anywhere in the world every two to three years. So we often said good-bye to friends. I taught my children that although they had to say good-bye to friends, they wouldn't have to say good-bye to their best friends, because they lived with them under the same roof. This concept took some time to sink in, but eventually they got the message.

Besides being friends with one another, we also learned to talk about our problems instead of letting them fester. We often had family meetings where the rules were simple: First state the problem without attacking the person. Second, listen while the other person spoke. If there were offenses, we would reconcile, then pray.

When the children were small, Vernon and I made it clear we wanted them to understand that Jesus must always feel welcomed in our home. To facilitate this, we had to learn to check our attitudes. We called it "Attitude Check." A friend showed us how this worked and we adopted it. Basically, whenever a family member acted un-Christ-like, another family member could yell out "Attitude Check!" The person with the attitude had to respond by saying, "Praise the Lord!" If their attitude were really bad, then they would have to lift both arms and shout, "Praise the Lord!" Of all the things Vernon and I tried, this was by far the best when the kids were younger. It also worked for us.

Keeping drama out of your home and out of your heart is critical if you want your marriage to be blessed. When you commit yourself to becoming the peacemaker and the promoter of unity and harmony in the home, you serve Satan his eviction notice.

Living Drama Free

It took several years of marriage for Vernon and I to

learn to live in harmony with one another. We had our relapses — his indifference and my defiance would creep in every once in a while — but for the most part we made a concerted effort to live without drama. The fact is that this is an on-going process. You are never without the potential for drama. There is always something pulling at our old natures. Please understand that as long as you live and desire to become the person God created you to be, you will always discover new areas of your old nature that you will sometimes have to find to control. But God uses these experiences to give you and your spouse opportunities for growth in your characters. God is interested in shaping you from the inside out, and the outside in. He will use whatever it takes to transform us into his glorious sons and daughters. Part of that shaping is to make you a completely whole. God understands the practicality of marriage. He knows that as long as we are in this body, we must work hard to be pleasing to one another. It has taken years for God to refine my attitude and to help me understand my husband. My desire is for God to polish me to the point that I can outwardly present what He is accomplishing inwardly.

CHAPTER 6
Irresistible Womanhood

"Every man wants to know he is a champion in his wife's eyes," Dr. E. B. Herman said, at a conference in Fayetteville, North Carolina in 1997. "Every man wants to know they win the trophy at home."

Walking out of the church that evening, I thought about how I could creatively convey this sentiment to Vernon. He has always been my champion, but I had never told him so, even after being married to him now for a little over 25 years. Let me explain something about Vernon. My husband is really gracious toward me. In my ministry, I often travel, which causes me to be on the road quite a bit. Yet, he is so supportive and patient. He often joins me in the ministry, though there are instances he frees me to travel even when that means I won't be home sometimes. Every man wants his wife to be home when the lights go out at night. But my husband makes those sacrifices for me so my ministry will run smoothly. I find it endearing that Vernon is willing to be a helper to me. I appreciate him and his commitment to seeing that I continue to do God's work.

So, when I got back from the conference, the Lord gave me the idea to buy Vernon a trophy — literally.

When I got to the store, I told the sales clerk that I wanted the tallest trophy she had. The tallest was 3 feet, so I took that one. I told her the trophy was to express to my husband that he was a true champion in my eyes. She looked at me real strange as if to say, "This will be very interesting." I described to her what Vernon means to me. On the trophy I wrote the following: "The Champ. You are my champion. Mr. Wonderful. Because you always come through for me."

As I described what I wanted, I could tell the woman was deeply moved. I paid for my trophy and went home to present it to Vernon. Now, as life would have it, when I returned home, Vernon started acting really strange and in ways that didn't deserve this trophy. I almost backed out. However, I had learned that doing for Vernon is doing for God. So, I can't base my actions according to whether I believe Vernon deserves my affection, time, or love. I do for him because I love God and I obey God. So, in this instance, no matter how much Vernon had acted contradictory to what I had inscribed on the trophy,   he was getting this trophy.

Upon presenting it to him, Vernon took a deep breath and exhaled slowly. His face softened into a look of little boy wonderment. He whispered, "I've never in my life received a trophy before."

Vernon reminded me that while attending Catholic school, he had not participated in sports. Although my husband loved to golf, fish, and camp, he had never been one for competitive sports. He never played basketball, or football, in high school; therefore, there had simply been no opportunity to receive a trophy.

I was stunned. It had never crossed my mind to do this for him before. Yet, it was obviously so important to him! I realized right then how much men need their wives to celebrate them. I think this is why they play sports. Men need cheerleaders in their lives — people who pump them up when life outside the home beats them down. So ladies, dust off your pom-poms and become the President of your husbands' fan clubs! Teach your children to celebrate their father! A woman who honors, respects, and admires her husband is a woman who is irresistible indeed.

From that moment on, I decided I would find ways to celebrate Vernon and try to live life in such a way that I constantly appreciate and thank him for what he does for me. Celebrating my husband as a champion completely opened my eyes and my heart.

My husband so loved the trophy that it sat on the dining room table for about six months. Eventually I told God, "OK Lord, I get the message."

Become Irresistible

Ladies, let me clue you in on a little secret. If you want to hang on to your man for the long haul, become the woman he can't live without. Be his confidant, his lover, and his prayer partner, but most of all, learn to truly understand his mind.

I learned many years ago that Vernon would open his heart to me when I asked him questions that demanded real answers and then waited for the answers without interrupting him. He loved it when I sought his advice and took it, or at the very least seriously considered it. He would smile every time I thanked him for doing the little things that brought me joy and made my life easier. I got more work done around the house when I praised his efforts and refrained from criticizing his execution.

Encouraging our husbands brings them closer to us. In fact, it means the difference between our husbands facing the world feeling like chumps or them facing the world feeling like champs. To confirm my findings, a sister friend of mine told me a story of how her grandmother would always tell her grandfather "You are such a nice man." When he would hear this a knowing smile would always light up his face.

To get our husbands to this place requires us to be irresistible women. An irresistible woman is a woman who loves God, prays often, meditates and practices the Word, and knows when to leave the spiritual realm in order to be a suitable helper to her partner in every area of his life.

We bring God the greatest amount of glory in our marital relationships when we are helpers. We are designed to be caregivers and nurturers whether or not we are living in a marital relationship. This is evident in our friendships with men. It is also evident when we care for our nieces and nephews, mentor neighborhood children, reach out to single women on our jobs or at our churches, or care for elderly neighbors, relatives, or family friends.

When God created woman, He created us with the purpose of being a compassionate vessel in which our husbands would find rest, rejuvenation, encouragement, and safety. Proverbs 31 is a beautiful example of one type of irresistible woman. *"Who can find a virtuous wife? For her worth is far above rubies. The heart of her husband safely trusts her; So he will have no lack of gain,"* (Proverbs 31:10-11). In this Scripture, the wife is described as a woman of valuable worth because she is compared with one of the most precious and rare jewels known to man. She is also seen as someone in whom her husband entrusts with his life. This alone testifies that an irresistible woman is one in whom her husband can share his heart and know without a shadow of a doubt that she has his back in this life.

What a Man Finds Irresistible

But don't take my word for it. Let's look at what one single associate pastor has to say. I led a conference in Dallas, Texas a few years ago where it wrapped up with a Question and Answer session. Former Senior Pastor E. K. Bailey, who has since gone home to be with the Lord, brought in one of his associate pastors, Marcus King — who is now an associate pastor at Friendship West in Dallas, Texas — so he could give a perspective from a single man's point of view. The question: "What is it that a single man looks for when he chooses a mate?" Here is what he said:

❖ "When a man looks for a wife, someone he is going to make his life partner, he looks for someone, first of all, who loves God. This is an irresistible trait to a godly man. He looks to see if your love for God is evident. It's not the braiding of the hair or the wearing of gold, but it's a woman who loves and fears God. This is an irresistible woman.

❖ "Not only does she love God, but she knows how to pray. She's a woman who can enter the presence of God and intercede. A godly man knows if he's going to succeed, if he's going to advance in the Kingdom of God, he needs a helper. He needs someone who can lock arms with him and pray with him. He needs a wife who has a prayer life. He needs a wife who can stand in the gap and intercede and plead for help on his behalf. A man wants a woman who can help him, not by doing what he is supposed to be doing, but to stand with him, to pray and encourage him.

❖ "He wants a woman who can handle the Word of God, who knows the book."

❖ So far so good, I thought. He asked for the right things: a man wants a woman who loves God; he wants a woman who knows how to pray; and he wants woman who fears God. Sounds good right? Then he closed with the following twist.. He said,

❖ He also wants a woman who knows how, when

she comes home, to put that Bible down and get it on.

The women just screamed. The place went into an uproar. Most of them totally understood where Marcus was coming from. However, some were offended at his candidness and walked out. I told the crowd that being sexually uninhibited in a marriage union is totally OK because God created sex to be a married couple's wedding gift — and we all know that God calls His creations good.

So if you are single, your desire should be to be godly, fear the Lord, have a strong prayer life, and be able to handle the Word. Of course, you want to wait until you get married before you enter into an intimate relationship with a man. So, I would say even to the single woman that you too should be irresistible.

In addition to these qualities, an irresistible woman must be a suitable helper to her husband. As wives, it is our job to discover our husbands' needs and to meet them — even before they know they have a need. Their needs could include order in their homes, a hot meal when they come from work, and someone to affirm them.

Now, we know his first basic need is God; the Word; and someone to pray for him, over him, and with him. We also know he needs someone who is sexually healthy. But what else does he need?

Our husbands need wives who know their worth and are secure with who they are so they can support them in what God has called our husbands to do. Women get this into your spirits: In order for you to be a suitable helper to your husband, you must understand how God looks at you and what He thinks of you, who you are in Christ, and the person of the Holy Spirit and His role in your life.

My Thoughts Are Higher Than Your Thoughts

I saw this film once. I can't remember the title, but it went something like this: In this particular village was a farmer with two daughters. One daughter was simply beautiful, and the farmer knew he could get a handsome bride price for her. At the time, the bride price of choice was cows. The more cows a man was willing to give for a woman, the more her worth. The farmer had no doubt in his mind that this daughter would bring him at least four or five cows. Now the other daughter was not beautiful at all, and the farmer believed he would get nothing for her. Because of this belief, he often treated this daughter with disdain. He never spoke kindly to her, he never praised her, or looked at her in a lovingly way. Because of this treatment, her sister's treatment was just as cruel and so was the treatment of the other women in the village.

Each day, the women would gather at the well. The women whose husbands paid a handsome bride price for her would go first dipping her bucket in the well. As you can imagine, the less than beautiful daughter would always go last.

As life would have it, one day a young man appeared at the farmer's doorstep. He was smitten you see and wanted one of the daughters as his wife. Well, the custom went that the two men would go for a walk and bargain on the bride price. Then once agreed upon, the young man in question would offer his beloved a gift as a promise of their betrothal. Then, he would go back and earn the money to pay the bride price. The young man goes to the farmer and they talk. The farmer, assuming the young man was interested in his beautiful daughter, starts out negotiations for six cows. The young man says to the farmer, "I'll give you eight cows for your daughter." Shocked and overwhelmed, the farmer readily agrees. Then the young man

77

reveal to him which daughter he just paid for — the other daughter! Now the farmer is flabbergasted. "The unattractive daughter," he thinks. "He wants the unattractive daughter? Amazing!"

As a gift, the young man had sent off to America for an ornate face mirror, comb, and brush because he had heard that the young woman didn't own such luxuries. When he presented his gift to her, she was overwhelmed with joy and cried. He promised to be back, and then left.

His gift flooded her heart. No one had ever cared about her appearance. In fact, she had gotten to a place where she didn't care either. Over the years the young woman had begun to believe everything people said about her. Their assessment of her worth became her assessment of herself. She didn't know any different because she never had anything of her own to see her own reflection. She only owned a broken pocket mirror, and the times she would go to the river, the water was so murky that the image staring back her was blurred.

But something miraculous happened. News of her bride price spread like wildfire in the village. Soon, when the women gathered at the well they stepped back because her bride price was far more than any of theirs. By stepping back, they gave her a new status among them. She was now first and not last.

Her beloved's gift of a mirror, comb, and brush inspired the young woman to take inventory of her appearance. Now that she had a new status, she needed a new look. She would often comb and brush her hair until it shown like the sun. She applied makeup that enhanced her beauty. She learned to walk with her head up and not have it fall in her chest. She sewed clothes that accentuated her body and not hide it.

When her beloved returned with the eight cows and was ready to claim his bride, he didn't recognize her. His gift had transformed her from the inside, out and the outside, in. She glowed. She floated. She was completely regal.

I tell this story because sometimes, as women, we have been seeing ourselves through others' damaging assessments.

In order to be an irresistible woman, we must see ourselves through the One who loves us unconditionally. I truly learned this lesson after studying Psalm 139. There it says that I am fearfully and wonderfully made. His thoughts toward me are precious and great. Everyday when I awake from slumber, God stands at the foot of my bed welcoming me back to Him.

Reading that made me realize how much God takes a personal interest in His creations. We are neither accidents nor mistakes. That same Psalm says that God wrote our days at the beginning of time before we had lived one of them; therefore, He planned and prepared for us to be here.

Understanding this allowed me to see myself the way God sees me. According to God, I am perfect for His purpose. There is a reason He made me in this form, in this time, and for this season. As women, we must stop accepting others' negative views of our worth and believe in only what our heavenly Father says of us. My grandmother used to say, "God doesn't make junk." If this is true, why would we believe the junk that others say about us? Ladies, learn to recognize unchangeable attributes and circumstances about your lives and get to a place of total acceptance. If the shape of your body resembles your mother's, love it. If you were brought up in the projects or trailer parks, so be it. We can't change those things. So instead of feeling shame, rejoice. Know that every experience we go through shapes our character.

A truly irresistible woman can embrace her total self. She can stand in the mirror naked and marvel at God's handiwork. But most importantly, an irresistible woman is comfortable in her skin.

After we understand how God sees us, we must

understand who we are in Christ. According to Colossians 1:12-22, through Christ we have a spiritual inheritance. We've been delivered from the power of darkness, we've been redeemed through His blood, our sins have been forgiven, we've been reconciled onto Him, and by His blood we have peace with God. Therefore, Jesus will present us to the Father holy, blameless, and above reproach. Bottom line ladies, we are complete in Jesus, (Colossians 2:10).

All this becomes solidified when we allow the Holy Spirit to work in our lives. Before Jesus left the disciples He said he would send a helper to dwell with them and within them. As children of God, that same Holy Spirit is available to us. In 1 Corinthians 6:19-20 it says, *"Or do you not know that your body is the temple of the Holy Spirit who is in you, whom you have from God and you are not your own? For you were bought at a price; therefore glorify God in your body and in your spirit, which are God's."* By inviting Jesus into our lives, we also invite the Holy Spirit to be a helper to us in times of need. The Holy Spirit is our comforter (John 14:16), our helper (John 16:7), our teacher (John 14:26), our guide (John 16:12-13) and our power (Acts 1:8). Once we understand what we house within ourselves how could we not know that we are irresistible women? Look at this way, if you are ever confused by your worth think about what Jesus paid to give you everlasting life. The price one is willing to pay for a thing determines its true value and He paid an enormous price for you.

Other Godly Irresistible Traits

Having a helpmate who knows who she is and her worth helps him become the man he was meant to become because she challenges him to step up. She challenges him to dig deep within himself and reach for excellence. Around her, he won't be able to settle for mediocrity. I once heard someone say, *"A good woman will make a man want to be a man."* A woman who knows her worth is sure to help her husband accomplish great things.

A man also needs someone who will follow his lead. He needs a woman who knows how to submit. As we learned in chapter 3, the first person a woman submits to is to the Lord. Submitting to God is an act of trust. If we first learn to trust God, then we'll be able to trust and submit to our husbands. The Bible says, *"Wives, submit to your own husbands as unto the Lord,"* (Eph. 5:22). My definition of submission is "to accept and support another person's mission to help bring it into fruition." I learned this as a military wife traveling with Vernon from country to country and from station to station. I had to be willing and ready to leave a home when the assignment was over. I had to be willing to pack up and move on when he said it was time to go.

Knowing how to submit doesn't take being married. If you are single, you learn to submit to your parents, mentors, job supervisors, church elders, or anyone with whom you have a teacher/student relationship. Being able to submit doesn't take away from your person-hood. In fact, submitting teaches you how to be humble and how to willingly serve in love. The Bible says we are to serve God with gladness. (Psalms 100:2). If we learn to do what the Lord says without hesitation and in full trust, we'll be able to do the same for our husbands knowing we are doing it to please God and not to please our husbands or to gain a favorable response.

Another aspect of being irresistible is becoming a wise woman who possesses a quiet spirit and the ability to be quick to hear yet slow to speak. The Bible even agrees, *"[She] who has knowledge spares [her] words, and a [woman] of understanding is of a calm spirit,"* (Proverbs 17:27). Wisdom in Hebrew means "sachal" or to be prudent, intelligent, instructed or to understand. Sachal is actually an entire thought process that occurs when one observes, ponders, reasons, learns, and reaches a conclusion. A wise woman always observes the situation before opening her mouth. As she watches, she thinks about what she hears and what she sees. Then she tries to create some type of order in her mind. After believing she has a grasp of the situation, she asks questions of those involved. Their answers ultimately inform her conclusions, then and only then will she offer any opinion. A wise woman understands that for this to work, she must hold her tongue and speak only when she understands all the facts. This becomes critical in times of danger and when quick thinking is necessary.

Sister, Hook Up the Package!

Ever wonder why men like women who look pulled together? It's not just because men are turned on by what they see. It's because her outward appearance says to the world she's strong, confident, knows her worth, and if she's Christian, then she also says the God she serves is mighty and powerful. A pulled together woman tells the world her husband is a good lover, good provider, a man of substance, and a man who makes her happy. How we face the world reflects upon our mates and reflects upon the God we serve.

"A woman with a sad, long face is a public rebuke to her husband" is an old saying that carries much truth. When we look bad we tell the world our husbands are not good lovers, they don't make us happy, and we live with them, but our lives are horrible. We also tell the world that we serve the Lord, but find no pleasure in Him.

82

Look at it like this: When you live a life without the joy of the Lord and find no reason to rejoice, then your countenance doesn't shine. When there's no radiance coming forth from you, you tell the world that you have no hero. The type of radiance I'm describing can't be purchased from Mary Kay, Revlon, or MAC. This radiance comes from a spirit that feeds on the Word of God and hopes in the Lord with full expectation. Without this radiance you tell people that you are a poor witness. "This God I serve brings me no pleasure. He doesn't hold my interest. He doesn't provide my basic needs." If you feel this way about God, think about what you communicate to the world about your husband.

So ladies get it together. Drink the Word. Fill your heart with God's love. Allow the spirit to shine through you. Open your hands and allow God to fill them with hope, love, expectation, joy, mercy, and peace. Then, dress the part. Show the world outwardly how good God is and how much of a blessing your husband is to you.

Men find women attractive if they are sensitive to the things they like. If your husband likes the natural look, wear the natural look. But do understand they may say one thing and actually like something else. So watch his eyes when a woman who looks completely pulled together with make-up, hair, nails and a dressed in a complementary outfit walks past. Take your cues from his reaction. This is why I take Vernon shopping with me. Most women want to look good for other women. But when you're married, you need to look good for your husband so he can enjoy the irresistible creation God called you to be.

Be All God Intends

Learning how to be everything that God intends prepares us for the times when our husbands are not everything

83

that God needs them to be. When we are strong and pulled together, our husbands are challenged to step up to the plate and become men of God. This takes time, patience, and love. But the end result is worth the effort.

Over the course of almost 30 years, God had taught me principle after principle — step by step. But the one principle that wasn't step-by-step was the principle of supernatural love. The Lord taught this between every other principle learned. Sometimes it would entail swallowing my pride to allow the family to get what they needed. Sometimes it meant changing my dreams in order for my husband to achieve his. Sometimes it meant doing things to please my husband and family that maybe I didn't necessarily enjoy just to make them smile.

God taught me that sacrificial/unconditional love, or agape in Greek, is the love that binds a marriage through the years. If I wanted to stay married to Vernon, I had to learn to love him with a supernatural love that went beyond my emotions, my mental capacity, and my own soul.

CHAPTER 7
Supernatural Love

Vietnam was over. Many of our Christian friends in the military were leaving that life behind to go back to school, go into the ministry, or just home. Those of us who survived had our whole lives ahead of us — most of us were only 22. Vernon and I were probably the oldest at 26 in 1978. Change was the buzzword around the Californian base.

Vernon and I talked about going, too. We were so grateful to be spiritually alive that we really wanted to share God's love with others. We were inspired to go into ministry because the people who taught us about God were missionaries. Their lives fascinated us. We liked the idea of using our gifts to help others learn about God. The whole idea of leaving the military and working for God excited Vernon and me. I pictured myself still traveling, but with a different purpose. No longer would we get our assignments from Randolph, the U.S. Air Force headquarters in Texas that decided when and where an airman was needed. Military personnel sent Randolph their requests for their dream assignments. Sometimes Randolph granted your choice in assignment. Other times Randolph sent airmen where they were critically needed because of skill level.

I was ready to get my assignments from God Himself in the form of missionary work. Vernon was too. We planned the classes we'd take and how we'd raise the children in the midst of our studies.

While I was busy dreaming, Vernon had a change of heart; he had decided to stay in the Air Force. I don't know if it was the third baby that concerned him. When I asked him, he wasn't quite sure himself. He just knew it was what he had to do. I looked at him. My mind screamed that I wanted out, and yet I knew he wouldn't make a decision like this if he hadn't turned it over in his mind a thousand times. Vernon and I had come a long way in terms of trust and understanding, so instead of going into my usual mind tirade, I told him I would pray about it.

I went and had some quiet time with the Lord. During our talk, the Lord said to me "Pat, submit to Vernon and be a suitable helper. Trust Me, support Vernon, and be there for him without resentment or disappointment. Let go of your idea on how to serve My kingdom. I can use Randolph. Commit to Vernon's decision out of your love for Me."

What did "out of my love for God" mean? I told Vernon I'd pray on it. Later on during my quiet time with the Lord, I came across the following Scripture:

"This is now the third time Jesus showed Himself to His disciples after He was raised from the dead. So when they had eaten breakfast, Jesus said to Simon Peter, 'Simon, son of Jonah, do you love Me more than these?' He said to Him, 'Yes, Lord; You know that I love You.' He said to him, 'Feed My lambs.' He said to him a second time, 'Simon, son of Jonah, do you love Me?' He said to Him, 'Yes, Lord; You know that I love You.' He said to him, 'Tend my sheep.' He said to him a third time, 'Simon, son of Jonah, do you love Me?' Peter was grieved because He said to him the third time, 'Do you love Me?' And he said to Him, 'Lord, You know all things; You know that I love You.' Jesus said to him, 'Feed My sheep.'" — John 21:14-17

This well-studied Scripture arrested my heart and mind. For the first time it no longer spoke to me about Peter. Now, it spoke to me about me. I understood what God meant. I now had to love Vernon with an unconditional love that surpassed my emotions and met his needs. I went to Vernon and said that I would support his decision to make the military his career. He hugged me and his face lit with joy. This was my first lesson in agape love.

I Love You Because I Love Him

Agape is the Greek word describing a kind of love that is unconditional and sacrificial. God demonstrated this type of love when He sacrificed His only Son for our salvation and redemption, (John 3:16). This is the type of love God was asking me at age 26 to display to my husband. Agape requires a sacrifice that is personally inconvenient. My sacrifice was letting go of my dream to go to Bible College and become a missionary. As Vernon and I grew in our marriage, I later understood why he wanted to stay in the military. At that time, he didn't see a way for us to be taken care of financially as a family plus go to school plus travel all over the world spreading the Good News. To Vernon, his first priority was making sure the family was completely covered. That for him outweighed any personal dream. Through this revelation, God showed me that Vernon and I would face other sacrifices that would be personally inconvenient and yet made for the good of the family vision.

It's like the Scripture about Peter. In the previous passage, the Lord was not asking Peter if he loved Him with his heart. He was asking Peter if he loved Him enough to let the desires of his flesh die for the greater good of all. The Lord wanted to know Peter's level of commitment to his covenant relationship with Him. Peter, doubting his own commitment level because of the Last Supper, could not answer the Lord with such a strong statement. Instead, Peter declared his heart tender toward Jesus. The word Peter used to answer Jesus was phileo, meaning in Greek to care for or be tender toward someone.

From 14 to 23, I loved Vernon with phileo love. But in 1978, God challenged me to take my love for Vernon to the next level. In order for my marriage to endure the decades, God wanted me to love Vernon sacrificially and unconditionally. Understand, I knew about sacrificial love. His was the love I had reserved for God. But in that moment, God showed me that the same love I had for Him, I now had to bestow upon Vernon; thus, began my triangle love affair with God, Vernon, and myself.

Love to Sacrifice

This triangle love affair challenged me to love Vernon with a reverent spirit, a quiet spirit, and a servant's spirit.

A reverent spirit is one that honors and reveres our husbands. In Esther 1:20 it says, *"When the king's decree, which he shall make, shall be published throughout all his empire — for it is great, all the wives shall give to their husbands honor — both to the great and to the small."* God would have us to revere our husbands whether they are men of great stature in the community or the church, or small in the sight of man. Every man ought to be king in his own house, and as wives we have the power to help establish their kingdoms.

In some homes, the father has his own special chair. This is where he reigns. Some fathers have their own special place at the head of the table. The kids know that's where Daddy sits. By 1983, I had developed this system. I made sure Vernon always sat at the head of the table. I didn't know that

88

the children understood Vernon's place in the family until the boys started competing to sit in their daddy's chair. I almost stopped them, but God said my sons should be trained to be kings as well. So on occasion, the boys took turns sitting in their dad's place when Vernon wasn't home. Now, as God would have it, LaVette also wanted to sit in her daddy's chair, but Vernon Jr. and Jevon teased her about this, saying that it was silly of LaVette to want to sit at the head of the table. In fact my oldest son, Vernon Jr., declared that girls weren't allowed to sit in their father's seat.

LaVette was crushed. God nudged me to use this opportunity to teach her how to revere her father. So I said to my daughter, "It's necessary, LaVette, for them to learn to be leaders. Let them have that place. We'll do some other things. There are other benefits to being a female."

By showing LaVette how to revere her dad, I was also teaching her the benefits of being a queen in training. I wanted her to understand that as Vernon's daughter, he would provide for her, protect her, make her feel special, nurture her gifts and talents, and give her wise godly counsel. When she saw her father as that type of man, and she experienced his love for her as a queen in training, she would be equipped with the understanding of what to look for in a potential husband.

A quiet spirit is one that crucifies the flesh and totally trusts in God. In 1 Peter 3:4, Peter says God considers a gentle and quiet spirit precious. When I looked further, the Greek word used to express gentle and quiet is the same word for lowly, which expresses the idea of one having the power of humble wisdom and penetrating love under perfect control.

In marriage, you must be a partner who daily crucifies your personal desires for the good of the family through the art of compromise. You won't always get your way. However, in a balanced marital partnership, you will always have a say in the decisions being made. If you speak your mind in humble godly wisdom, you will influence your family to make sound choices based on godly counsel. The ability to function in this capacity requires self-control. You can't fly off the handle at the drop of a hat because you didn't get what you wanted, or someone didn't take your advice. You have to be a woman who is able to speak her mind so she is heard, and has the grace to step aside if the advice isn't taken. The grace that allows you to step aside is because your trust lies in God. You can do this because you know that no matter the decision made or the ultimate outcome, all of it will be for your good and God's glory. God taught me this lesson the hard way. He used my defiant attitude to show me what not to do.

Let me state for the record that I am not a morning person. However I have always tried to be nice to my family in the morning. Even if I woke up with an attitude, I learned not to argue. Instead, I would hold my tongue until they came home for lunch in the afternoon, or came home from school or work in the evening. I understood that if I stepped back from my own emotions, I would be able to look at the situation rationally, and then be able to speak to people with self-control in tact.

One fall morning in 1983 didn't happen like that. I don't remember why I was angry, but I specifically remember this morning because I was so out of character I scared myself. Instead of waking up peaceful, I woke up in a foul mood. I went straight off. I had a complete fit. I fussed and argued with Vernon while the kids were getting ready for school. I was "having my say." The kids left for school with long, concerned faces. But my wrath wasn't quenched. I shouted at Vernon all while he dressed and walked to the car to go to work. In fact, I stood in the doorway going into football coach mode letting him know I was not pleased. "Do you understand me?! Did you hear everything I said?"

Without looking at me, he answered dryly, "Yeah, yeah, yeah. Yeah, yeah, yeah."

When the car door slammed, I folded my arms across my chest in a self-righteous posture and told the Lord, "Now Lord, get him. While he's at work, get this across to him."

At this point of the day I would normally have my quiet time with the Lord. But I couldn't approach the Word, much less study. In fact, I walked right past my Bible. I thought, "OK, Lord, I know I need to get in the Word, but I have to settle down."

God said, "No, come now." When I sat down, God asked me, "Was it worth it to have your say this morning? The way your family left here, was that really worth your sayWas it worth it to see them go out the way they went out? To know the atmosphere that you created — was it worth it?"

Thinking back on their long, sad, and concern-filled faces I realized my say that morning wasn't worth it. Not only did I send them out with hurt feelings, but I also ruined an opportunity to allow God to minister to Vernon and me. That morning I forgot to trust God. I had not asked Him to handle the situation in the way He saw fit. Instead of trusting God, I took matters into my hands and created an atmosphere of chaos.

Being able to control your emotions is also an aspect of agape love. Sometimes, your pride is the sacrifice you pay to maintain peace in your home. The Word says, *"Pride goes before destruction; and a haughty spirit before a fall,"* (Prov. 16:18). My pride got in the way of God's ability to minister to Vernon and me. Because of my decision to "have my say," my family's day was disrupted before they ever left the house. Had I crucified my pride and kept silent that morning, my family would have left the house in complete peace, and I would have had a chance to re-evaluate my feelings, then I could have spoken to Vernon with clarity and in a spirit of truth and love.

A servant's spirit is one that serves the Lord in complete zeal. In Romans 12:11 it says, we are to love one another by being *"fervent in spirit; serving the Lord."* You serve the Lord with gladness and joy. You serve completely and without holding back. You give your all—everything within you—to ensure the needs of the people God has asked you to serve are met. This is a sacrificial action, because when you serve, your personal needs and desires are not the focus.

This description calls to mind the woman with the alabaster box in Luke 7:36-50. Jesus was in the house of the Pharisees, and their custom was to bring in a slave to wash the guests' feet. In those days, the roads were dusty and it was a simple courtesy, to have someone wash the feet. It would be like offering our guests a glass of water. But the day Jesus came, no one had offered Him that courtesy. Instead, they sat and talked.

The Bible says a woman, who everyone knew as a sinner, came in uninvited. She approached Jesus, knelt down at his feet, and cried. Her tears washed the dirt and grime from His feet. She then dried his feet with her hair. After she cleansed and wiped Jesus' feet, she anointed his feet with the perfume from the alabaster jar; thus, preparing Jesus for burial. God put this story in the Word to be a memorial of her servant spirit. This is the humility with which we need to serve our spouses.

The time I serve Vernon the most is at meals. He likes his food to look pretty. When dinner is visually pleasing, he'll say, "Ooh, everything looks nice and colorful." If I'm in a hurry and forget, then the food doesn't look as appetizing, and he'll say, "Hey, hey slow down. Now when I serve you I always make sure your food is nice and colorful." The worst insult to him is to slap food on his plate and serve it to him. The way the food is fixed and presented sends him a message. It can either say, "I enjoy serving you. I honor you." Or, when I forget it says, "Serving you is a chore. I do not honor you." It's not enough that we serve. We must be mindful of our attitudes while we serve.

When Jesus served us, He did it with humility. Before He went home to the Father, He told His disciples to serve each other the way He had served them, (John 13:13-17). In this passage, Jesus was talking about being a servant leader. I see the passage also touching upon the relationship between a husband and wife. When we serve one another with humility, we sacrifice our inclination to be self-centered. Instead, we become God-centered in the respect that God can use us minister to one another. Agape love is not self-centered or self-seeking. It is the type of love that seeks to meet the needs of those we love despite their timing or convenience in our lives.

God Rewards Service

Over the years, I have learned that loving Vernon God's way has saved me from many a heartache and headache. It has taken time, but the rewards have been more than worth the efforts. Together he and I have weathered storms and witnessed triumphs. Becoming a woman with a reverent, quiet and servant's spirit was not a simple road to take. But I was determined to obey God in all things. I was determined to love my Lord with my obedience. In doing so, I can honestly say my marriage is healthier and stronger for it.

Getting to this place often meant postponing personal dreams and goals. It meant not becoming attached to a certain home or even a city. It meant making do with very little sometimes. But I have almost 35 years with my husband. I wouldn't trade that for the world. I decided a long time ago my marriage and my family had to come first. Once I had committed those to areas of my life to God, every decision I made had them in mind.

The principle of sacrificial love permeated every aspect of my marriage, especially my intimate relationship with Vernon. Now that he and I had learned how to be emotionally, mentally, and spiritually naked with each other, God taught us that intimacy can be passionate and holy when experienced as a ministry.

Chapter 8
Ministry of Intimacy

"Rise up my love, my fair one and come away. For lo, the winter is past, the rain is over and gone. The flowers appear on the earth; the time of singing has come. And the voice of the turtledove is heard in our land. The fig tree puts forth her green figs, and the vines with the tender grapes give a good smell. Rise up, my love, my fair one, and come away!" — King Solomon to the Shulamite woman, Song of Solomon 2:11-13

"My beloved is mine, and I am his." — The Shulamite woman to King Solomon, Song of Solomon 2:16

The first one came on Feb. 1, 1980: A card from Vernon with words scratched out and replaced with words from the Song of Solomon. The line from Song of Solomon 1:8 *"...oh fairest among women..."* anchored the card, and he signed it, *"Love Always, Versolomon."*

More cards came — anniversary, Mother's Day, Christmas, Easter, and later "just because."

Versolomon...humph. This was Vernon's romantic side slipping out and gently kissing me on the cheek. *Versolomon* didn't make an appearance until 10 years after Vernon and I had been married. This is 1980. God had resurrected our marriage just 4 years before, and gradually from then to now we invested in our marriage by going to marriage encounters that gave us tools to help us strengthen our emotional and physical intimacy.

When Vernon and I first got together, I thought I knew romance. I mean he had wined, dined, spoiled, and completely pampered me. But it wasn't until after we gave ourselves to Christ that I experienced romance, love, and passion from a holy and sacred perspective. It wasn't until then did I realize that true intimacy meant a holy union between my husband, our Lord Jesus Christ, and me. Intimacy is ministry when communion and the Word intermingle with the love between a husband and wife that is anchored in covenant relationship and surpasses human emotion.

Truly there is no greater wedding gift that God could have given couples than the gift of intimacy. Physical intimacy is the ministry of giving and taking, receiving and releasing, sharing and communication, and ultimate praise. It is a time when husbands and wives bond and become one flesh in a holy way. It is an experience of true service.

There is a an old saying, "We don't make love. We express the love we already have for one another." To me, this has always meant that when we as couples begin to see our love for each other as a ministry, then our marriages would surpass the legal binding recognized in the court of law. Our marriages would elevate to the place where patience really is a virtue and two-way communication is the norm. We'll come to our bedrooms with the attitude we're there to give and take.

Our minds and hearts will stay on our husbands and wives. The focus of physical intimacy will be pleasing one another as well as bringing our spouse complete pleasure and delight. We'll think, "I want you to glory and bask in the atmosphere of love." And, the love we have in our hearts for God will help us make that a reality.

God Calls Married Passion Holy

Thinking on those times still makes me smile with delight because I realize just how much God wants His married children to experience passion from a holy frame of reference. So often, passion is relegated to the young and unmarried. Their love is always hot, heavy, uncommitted, and short-lived. But God says passion should be tempered with endurance and that only can be found in a covenant relationship between a man and woman who are committed to a life of service and companionship to one another and to God.

Love is the greatest power on earth. It will move mountains and endure pain and hardship. Love is the force that keeps God tethered to us and us to Him. In Romans 8:35, Paul writes, *"Who shall separate us from the love of God?"* The answer? No one! This same love is the love that Christ has for the Church, which is why He willingly sacrificed Himself on the cross. Scripture says, *"For God so loved the world that He gave His only begotten Son, that whoever believes in Him should not perish but have everlasting life,"* (John 3:16). A love like this created the world and changes the world. A love like this strengthens a couple to go the distance in their marriage for as long as they both shall live.

Over the years, I have researched this book of the Bible and discovered that scholars differ as to what this poem truly illustrates. Is it a true depiction of the love Christ has for the

Church? Or, is it simply a poem describing the love between a man and woman? I believe you can use this book for both.

The Song of Solomon is also called   Song of Songs because it is the greatest song that has ever been sung. Sometimes the Bible qualifies something as being the best of the best by repeating it. For instance, when we read Lord of lords, it means that there is no lord greater than Jesus. He is the greatest Lord of all. When we hear the title of Jesus as being the King of kings, it means that there is no other king greater than King Jesus. Likewise when we say Holiest of holy, we're saying there is none holier. So Song of Songs means this song is the greatest love song of all.

The Song of Solomon is a poem that was put to music. It's the story of a love relationship between King Solomon and the Shulamite woman. The Song of Solomon expresses strong emotions of the heart made to affect the reader by stirring up our emotions, and delighting our senses. The song conveys the thrill that the physical senses enjoy. It is God's way of communicating to us what a holy relationship between a man and woman should resemble. It's also His way of showing us how to set the atmosphere for love and why it's necessary.

Holy Passions Appeals to the Senses

To set the atmosphere for love, one must discover ways to appeal to all of the senses — touch, smell, sight, hearing, taste, and soul.

"Let him kiss me with the kisses of his mouth,"(Song of Solomon 1:2). Here, kissing speaks of and relates to the desire for intimacy and pleasure between a husband and his wife. The lining of the lips and the skin around the lips is the thinnest skin exposed on the body. God made this area thin so

we will experience great pleasure when we are kissed. Therefore, I tell single men and women often that if they don't plan on having sex, don't kiss because it initiates the physical expression of sex. When you kiss a person and you are not married, especially when you kiss them on the mouth, you are defrauding them. To defraud means to wake up an appetite you cannot righteously satisfy. Kissing is the first step in physical connection, or foreplay.

When the Shulamite woman said she wanted to be kissed *"with the kisses of his mouth,"* she meant she wanted to be kissed over and over and over again. Her desire is for her lover to express great affection to her unceasingly.

Sex begins with affection. To a woman affection is the key to her heart. It creates an environment that frees her to respond to her husband's need for sex. When a woman receives affection, she is usually freer to finish a sexual union. In actuality, affection liberates women to express themselves sexually without inhibitions. However if there is no affection or foreplay, the sex act is cold and leaves the woman feeling frustrated, defiled, and used. But when a husband meets his wife's need for affection and attention, she'll respond by meeting his need for sex. Scripture says, *"Let the husband render to his wife the affection due her, and likewise also the wife to her husband,"* (1 Cor. 7:3).

One of the ways a man can meet his wife's need for affection is by touching her. Hold her hand. Stroke her back. Hug her. Pat her arm. Kiss her before leaving out for work. What's usually needed is a quick touch to show he is connected with her and paying attention. Besides touch, he can show her affection by giving her gifts — not necessarily expensive gifts. He can show her affection by listening to what she says, making eye contact with her, and taking her counsel once in a while. He can show her affection by playing with her.

I once told my husband foreplay to me is washing the dishes with me. Why? Because, when Vernon works with me we connect. We talk and play right there at the sink. We discuss each other's day, and we talk over decisions that need to be made concerning the house or children. We also flirt with each other. Washing dishes is a calming activity that allows us to be in each other's space and be aware of each other's moods and needs. Sometimes, just washing dishes allows me to concentrate on him. My mind focuses not on the dishes, but on Vernon.

Understand, ladies, a woman's sex organ is her mind. So when our husbands help us around the house, they say to us, "I'm sensitive to you. I'm paying attention to you. I appreciate you." When that kindness is demonstrated, it causes us to relax, think romantic thoughts, and be ready to respond to our husbands after we tuck the children in for bed.

Sharing a household chore is not the only way that helps prep our minds for physical intimacy with our husbands. Quiet time with the Lord and reading the Word is an excellent activity at the start of your day to help you set the atmosphere for love in your mind. In your prayer time, ask the Lord to cleanse your mind of all the clutter of the day-to-day worries, responsibilities, and chores. Pray this way, "Lord, today, sanctify my mind and help me tonight. I want to be responsive." By praying this, we ask God to free our minds so we will be completely in tune with our husbands when it is time to respond to them.

Sometimes we can't fully respond to our husbands because our minds are pulled in so many directions: the children, our husbands, our homes, our jobs, our church activities, our families, etc. There is no room for romance when the cares of the world monopolize your thoughts. But when you ask God to cleanse your mind of these cares and allow you to concentrate on pleasing and pleasuring your husband, as well as thoroughly enjoying the time you spend with him, you in essence ask God to prep your mind for love.

Physical intimacy is a two-way street. You can't just show up and lay there. It doesn't work like that. Men need more than a warm body underneath them. They need their wives to connect with them physically, mentally, emotionally, and spiritually in the bedroom. When you connect with each other on all four planes, you participate in the ministry of intimacy because you touch each other in places that need healing, understanding, validation, appreciation, and celebration. When this is accomplished, you both can end your lovemaking on a halleluiah note of praise thanking God for His wedding gift of intimacy.

Now if you really want to bless your husband and add spice to your sex life, be the initiator sometimes. Yes, it is natural that men are the initiators, but as I have read, as I have experienced, and as women have shared with me, men appreciate it when women initiate. They find that exciting and stimulating. If you really want to be an initiator, call your husband at work before he even gets home, and let him know what your plans are for the evening. I am not talking about telephone sex. Just plant a seed in your husband's mind to give him a sense of expectation as to what the evening is going to be like. This may not feel natural to you at first. But when you make up in your mind that married sex is holy, it pleases God, and you know that your needs can be met, then you can begin to initiate. So make up your mind, "I am going to be the initiator sometimes," and do so by preparing yourself. Reading good, excellent, clean books can help you. The Song of Solomon is one.

"For love is better than wine," (Song of Solomon 1:2). Here the bride says that when her beloved expresses love to her it

causes her to get caught up, be enraptured, and to completely forget everything else but him. His love has the same effect on her as wine — it intoxicates her. It causes her to act out of character. She's free. Their lovemaking, done in the marriage bed, is holy, undefiled, and better than wine.

I often minister to women who were sexually active before marriage. They had experienced hot, burning passion, or in this case lust, with their spouses as unmarried people. However, when the couple married, she found that for some strange reason they were not as hot and passionate for each other as they had been when they weren't married. When we break God's moral laws, we experience the consequences of not enjoying sex the way He intended. So I encourage you single women to wait on the Lord. But if you've already engaged in sexual activity, ask God to cleanse you then commit your body to the Lord and abstain from sex.

When I counsel singles, I tell them that because the sex drive is so strong, the only way to avoid that particular temptation is to flee from youthful lust and avoid the very presence of evil, (2nd Tim. 2:22). Great men of the Bible often fell when it came to their sex drives: David was spiritually strong and he fell; Solomon was intellectually strong and he fell; Samson was physically strong and he fell. Face it, it is not in our strength, but it is in our obedience to God and His word for us to avoid the lust trap. Maybe we can do what Joseph did. He is a perfect example of how we should respond to lust. He ran! (Gen. 39:5-12). So, if you want your marriage gift of physical intimacy to be better than wine — RUN!

In order to experience this, we need to set the atmosphere of our bedrooms. *"Thy name is as an ointment poured forth,"* (Song of Solomon 1:3). Here the word "ointment" speaks of perfume. At this time in history, it was a tradition in eastern culture that servants would release a fragrance in the banquet room while the king ate. Servants did this by pouring the fragrance from one vessel into the next. The fragrance created an atmosphere befitting of a king.

The oil was also used to anoint the king when he entered the room. Remember in John 12:1-3 when Mary of Bethany anointed Jesus' feet with a pound of expensive oil then dried his feet with her hair? By anointing Jesus' feet, Mary ministered to Jesus. Her act was an act of true worship. By doing this, she told everyone in the room that she recognized Jesus as the King. When we properly set the atmosphere of our bedrooms to receive our husbands, we are telling them they are the kings of our households.

To properly set the atmosphere means to reserve our bedrooms for lovemaking, resting and relaxing only. We don't chat with our girlfriends in our bedrooms. We don't allow clutter to seize a hold of our bedrooms. We don't treat our bedrooms as our office away from the office.

Our bedrooms are our sanctuaries — holy places. To help put us in that frame of mind, ladies, I encourage you pray a prayer of anointing over your bedrooms. Ask the Spirit of God to sanctify those rooms and make them holy. Ask Jesus to rule and reign in your bedroom as Lord of your bedroom. Pray it would not be defiled, and God would give you a healthy attitude toward your husband and your shared sex life. Pray you will be able to create an ambiance in your bedroom that is wholesome. Turn on soft music. Light candles. Put fresh linens on your beds. Make this room as special as possible, so it will be a place where serious ministering will be done. When you pay attention to your surroundings, your husband will definitely notice.

I am amazed that, although we have a phone in our Bedroom, my husband gets up and goes into another room to talk on the phone. It took the Lord to reveal to me that Vernon does this to reserve our room for us alone. We need to remember that the bedroom is his kingdom. This is his castle and it needs to be preserved.

Now ladies, what I am about to tell you may bother you and send many of you wanting to put this book down, but hear me out. We have to face the facts. Men are visual creatures so that means we have to look and smell good. Yes, I know there is more to us than meets the eye. But we must first get in the eye gate for them to see the deeper side of our beings.

We must appeal to all of their senses. Ladies, take your husbands shopping. Go to the fragrance counter and let him smell the colognes and perfumes. When he finds one that he likes, that's the one you buy for yourself. Even if you don't particularly like it, if he loves it, then you wear that one. But only wear that perfume at night. In psychology, the term is called classical conditioning. When you wear a certain perfume only in the evening or only at night, it gives him a subliminal message. If you wear a certain perfume only when you want to initiate sex with your husband, it tells him so, turns him on, and gets him ready.

Men respond to sight. So ladies don't go to bed looking crazy. Some of us go to bed like we're going hunting — heads wrapped up, and faces drab and plain. We should go to bed as a sight to behold, not run away from. Am I saying to go to sleep in make-up? No. But I am saying go to bed with enough make-up on to cause your husband to look at you and delight in you. Once you have ministered to him, you can remove the make-up if you wish.

Another thing — throw away all of your raggedy, faded gowns. Those T-shirts and flannel gowns must go! Yes, I know they are completely comfortable. I know they have been broken in just right. But they don't help set a stimulating atmosphere in the bedroom. Instead, buy some sexy lingerie.

The first time my husband bought me some lingerie, I didn't appreciate the gift. Vernon was stationed in Greenland. After six months he came home for a 30-day break. He had called me several times to let me know he had found the perfect gift for me in Sweden. So I'm pumped. I'm excited because he's excited. I was completely curious to see if this would be some kind of perfume or shoes or a purse or jewelry. You know something really just for me. Then when he came and presented his gift, I tore open the package and had to hold my face together. The man had bought me some nighties all the way from Sweden. They were pretty, but they were nighties! Here I am all excited trying to figure out what he could have found that I wouldn't have had Stateside, and the man buys me nighties! It took a friend of mine to show me that obviously these nighties were what Vernon wanted to see me in. Looking at the gift from Vernon's perspective changed my attitude. I realized that he wanted me to dress for him. So, I slipped on the nighties and proceeded to minister to my husband.

Men may not say it matters what you wear to bed, but it really does. I am not saying you have to go to *Frederick's of Hollywood* to buy lingerie. But I am saying you need to go to *Victoria's Secret,* or your favorite department store and buy a couple of nighties that look nice to sleep in so you can minister to your husband properly.

Not only do we need to appeal to what our husbands see, touch, and smell, but we must also appeal to their ear gate. Think about it. When we go into the presence of God, we come into His courts with thanksgiving and praise on our lips. We bless God's holy name. As wives, we need to use a similar principle when it comes to our husbands. Men respond to what they hear.

When you and your husband come into your bedroom chamber, you should have the spirit of gratitude. Speak words of kindness to him. Begin your foreplay with him by thanking him for being a good provider and a good protector. Thank him for his godly counsel. Remind him of the role he plays in your life, and how he's blessed you. Don't discuss the children during this time. Leave them out of this. Just concentrate on the two of you. Even if your husband is unsaved, you can come to him with gratitude and pride. He will respond to you. At first, he may be slow to adjust to your advances, but I promise you, it's the Lord's way. God honors His way, and your husbands will be honored as well.

" Setting the atmosphere" reminds me of Esther. Here was a young woman who found herself in the king's palace being prepared to possibly be the next queen of Persia. For a year, she was given oils, ointments, and other perfumes to prepare her body to receive the king. When her turn came, she was allowed to take any jewelry or clothing she wanted with her from the women's quarters. Instead, Esther asked Hegai, the king's eunuch and the person in charge of the women, what the *king* liked. He told her, and she wore it. Because she listened to Hegai, Esther found favor with King Ahasuerus. He fell in love with her, married her, and put a royal crown on her head.

When we treat our husbands as kings by honoring and serving them, they will respond to us by treating us royally and crowing us as their queens. My husband especially responds when I am sensitive to his needs. Being sensitive means understanding his moods. For example, I know when he's had a rather demanding day at work by a look on his face. At those times, I don't burden him with the problems of my day. I wait until he is ready to talk. I am patient and take my cues from him. I wait until I see that he is ready to share whatever is weighing on his heart, and then I listen very carefully. Because I wait, I free Vernon up to come home and get settled before having to deal with home issues. By being sensitive like this, my husband reciprocates, sometimes not in the way I expect, sometimes not when I expect, but he always reciprocates.

However, don't do these things for the reciprocation. Remember, we've discussed in earlier chapters that we do these things for our husbands to please God and in pleasing Him we in turn please our husbands. We must continually ask, "Lord, what pleases You?" This was Esther's request and her continual cry, "What will it take to please the king?" In the end, she was rewarded with a crown of her own.

Men are also turned on by taste. So young women, learn to cook, and my more mature ladies, don't stop cooking. Some of you may be asking, "What does food have to do with sex?" Everything. When a man pays attention to a woman, he's saying, "I want to give you affection." That, as we've learned, is foreplay. So, when a woman serves her husband his favorite meal with a sweet spirit and simple praise for all that he is to her, she's saying, "I know the things that you enjoy and I want to provide those things for you. I want to create an environment where you are experiencing pleasure with all of your senses and not just your sex organs." That is foreplay. Cooking his favorite meal also fills your home with good and delicious smells. You are creating a mood. You are setting the atmosphere for love.

Cultivating Green Marriage Beds

We've made ourselves smell and look beautiful to behold inside and out, we've sanctified our bedrooms with prayer and fragrance, and we've told our husbands they are our champions and our best friends, and we've cooked our kings a meal they will never forget. The atmosphere is set. The appetites have been whetted. Now physical intimacy can begin.

107

In Song of Solomon 1:16, the Shulamite woman describes her marriage bed as being green. Green represents life, freshness, growth, vigor, nourishment, and satisfaction. This is exactly what God wants us to experience in our relationship with our husbands. As the bed is holy, and as our bedrooms are holy sanctuaries, God wants us to experience freshness and renewal.

A normal, healthy sex life is where the married couple comes together, praying and asking God and the Holy Spirit to take control of that time. Ask God to give you the power enjoy the gift of sex. Then when you pray, you begin to communicate with your husband and your husband begins to communicate in return. During this time, communicate to him in a healthy way what feels good to you and what doesn't. If he's touching you in an area that irritates you or makes you feel unclean, definitely tell him. Men want to be known as great lovers. They take great pride and delight in knowing that they are bringing you pleasure.

When I say unclean, I mean if he touches you or asks you to do something that makes you feel defiled then tell him. You can defile your marriage bed by engaging in a sexual activity that makes you or your spouse feel used. This is perversion.

The Bible says that the bedroom is holy and undefiled. Some think this means that anything goes between a married couple. I don't believe that is the case. I believe that this passage means the bedroom is holy, therefore, don't defile it. There are ways that you can defile your bedroom. You can defile your bedroom by bringing in pornography, watching X-rated movies, and allowing and/or inviting third parties into your bedroom. You can defile it by simply doing something that on the surface seems very benign, and yet you are totally offended. Your husband may like sucking your toes, but you hate it. That is defilement to you. Defilement is all of these examples and everything in between.

Some people say they don't feel uncomfortable with perversion. If you are a growing Christian, I promise you that the Holy Spirit will show you what is healthy and what is unhealthy. God will sanctify your sex life. Then, in the midst of your intimate expression of love, the Holy Spirit will show you what is nourishing and fresh, and what is satisfactory and life giving. God is the controller of our lives and He will show us what is and what is not acceptable.

Earlier, I shared how my father told me that though I may have been very nervous about following my husband to Oregon, I needed to in order to keep the strange woman out of our lives. My father was also telling me that by being away from my husband too long my absence would incite my husband to lust. Scripture says that once we've married, our bodies are no longer our own. We cannot deny our spouses their due without the other's consent, (1 Cor. 7:4). This means if we feel God is calling us to a time of fasting and prayer, we need to abstain from sexual relations for a time. We must ask our spouses if this is OK with them. Once the fast is over, we are to come back together quickly so that *"Satan does not tempt you because of your lack of self-control,"* (1 Cor. 7:5).

These principles are meant to keep our marriage beds green and holy. God intended for his married children to enjoy one another freely and without shame. Remember sex is not a spectator activity. It is a time where two people who are deeply committed to one another can communicate on a whole different level. When sex becomes frustrating, it is either because there is a lack of communication or you may harbor some unhealthy attitudes about sex. These issues are only nipped in the bud when we become mature men and women.

A mature woman knows herself. She will know her pleasure areas and be able to communicate this knowledge to her husband in a loving way. She will know what excites her and what doesn't excite her. She will not leave her husband to fumble and try to find out. She will help him by responding to his touch. If something doesn't work, she'll say, "Baby, that's not working." She'll say it without making him feel inadequate. Then she'll guide him to the areas that bring her complete pleasure. When a man is mature, his desire is not just to experience pleasure, but that you would experience pleasure as well. In fact, if you can get up and go wash dishes or do some other chore, he did not accomplish his part of the experience. A good lover will make love to your spirit first, your mind second, and your body third. As a way to help each other discover those areas that please us the most, there are many good and healthy books and videos on the market geared toward couples from your local Christian bookstore.

The word "green" also represents rest. Remember in the 23rd Psalm where it speaks of our Shepherd making us lie down in green pastures? When husbands and wives respond to each other in the right way, we are refreshed and restored. We are able to relax in a place of delight. We are strengthened and renewed.

Stages of Physical Intimacy

There are three stages of physical intimacy — arousal, plateau, and recovery.

Arousal is the first stage. It is a time when your senses are completely awakened and when you are ready to respond to your husband and he to you. Arousal can occur with touches, looks, being embraced and kissing when it conveys tenderness. Normally, men don't have to prepare themselves to be aroused because arousal for them comes instantly. However, for us, we need preparation because our primary sex organ is the mind. Remember we talked about sanctifying our minds with prayer in the morning to prepare ourselves to respond to our husbands at night? Well before we start, we can we can invite our husbands to help us prepare our minds. We can ask them to cleanse us with *"the washing of water by the word,"* (Eph. 5:26). The Bible says that this is what our husbands are supposed to do as well because the Word of God cleanses us.

Many times a woman has a hard time being aroused in a healthy way because she has been defiled. Perhaps as a little girl she may have defiled herself with pornography or acts of perversion. She may have been molested, or was a victim of incest or rape. We also can defile ourselves by fornicating. Whatever the case, where there has been defilement it must be cleansed.

If you defiled yourself with fornication or perversion, ask God for forgiveness. "God, make this right. Purify me. Forgive me for defiling my relationship." Ask God to take you back and sanctify that which you have defiled by lowering your moral standards. Just ask God to forgive you: "Cleanse me, forgive me, sanctify me, make me whole again." He will begin a work.

Some of us have been molested or raped, and that's why we don't enjoy the gift. Satan gets a foothold in our relationships. We feel that we can't respond intimately to our husbands because of the deep violation we've experienced. But God is able. He can heal wounds so you can experience the joy of physical intimacy with your husband. To help you, ask God to change your view of this time with your husband. Ask God to help you see this time as a special time of worship. You can pray: "God, You said physical intimacy is Your gift to married people. You said it's good. You said this is what my marriage is supposed to give me. So, now Lord, would You please help me to experience this from Your perspective?" By asking God to come into the midst of your time with your husband, you've switched the focus from the physical act to a time of sharing hearts and becoming one flesh.

When a man is married to a woman who has been sexually violated, he will find she is either super turned on or super turned off. He can help her find a healthy sexual balance by ministering to her through his priestly role. He can sanctify her by reading the Word over her. He can prepare his wife by anointing her with oil, which is always representative of the Holy Spirit. Men, when you pray, let her hear the words you speak over her. As you read the Bible over her, the words will cleanse and prepare her for your time together. If you allow the Word to condition your mind as it relates to sexual intimacy, then when you ask God to take control over that time, He will.

The next stage of sexual intimacy is the plateau where our orgasms, or the sexual climaxes, are experienced. Frustration in making love is usually felt the most here. A woman needs intense stimulation to experience arousal in order to plateau. A man needs to control himself if they desire to experience a climax together, if they desire to experience orgasm together.

It is not critical or abnormal if a married couple doesn't experience their orgasm at the same time. There's nothing wrong with you. Men reach orgasm very quickly. Just as we steam up, they are cooling down. This is pure physiology. However, if a husband and wife want to experience an orgasm together, they must be in tune with each other and communicate what will help them get to that place. This type of timing takes practice and patience.

Also understand that just as our husbands can orgasm very quickly, it takes us a lot of energy to reach that point.

Oftentimes, the pressure of wanting to orgasm can take away the joy of the experience. My advice to you is instead of focusing on the orgasm itself, focus instead on wanting to express love to your husbands. Minister to their needs. Listen to how they respond to you when you touch them. If they say something feels really good, continue to do that which you are doing. And by the same token, allow him to pleasure you. Tell him what feels good to you. Let him know that a certain touch on a particular part of your body lights on you fire. Enjoy each other to the fullest. Don't hold back. By changing your focus on your husband's needs, the frustration of not reaching an orgasm doesn't spoil your time with each other.

For more information on experiencing an orgasm, read *Women's Orgasm* by Georgia Klein Garber. I offer this because many women have felt safe in reading this book and have gained a better understanding in how the body functions. Now the final stage is recovery, or the afterglow. This phase is typically most important to women. At this point we are completely open, vulnerable and willing to share. Because we are so open, it hurts us when our husbands just roll over and go to sleep. Instead, husbands take the time to have your wives lay in your arms. Enjoy talking and/or laughing. Sexual intimacy is a spiritual act that is expressed physically. When it is enjoyed in the right way, God blesses and sanctions it. When your mind is sanctified and clean, you can come to the place of recovery and your experience will be one of worship and praise. Your focus, even though you enjoyed each other physically, can be turned toward the Lord and you can end on a note of Hallelujah praise. You can enjoy the Lord together. You can bless God's name.

Extolling the name of the Lord is a sign of when real intimacy has taken place because there is nothing more intimate that you can do with your mate than pray together. By praying you do two things: One, thank the Creator for creating physical intimacy. Two, seal the experience as holy by asking God to bless your mate. When you enjoy each other fully, you don't just see the nakedness of their bodies, you see and experience the nakedness of their souls. Prayer allows you to experience the oneness and shamelessness Adam and Eve experienced in the Garden of Eden before for the fall. They were always naked before God. There was nothing in their relationship that happened that He didn't see. When we ask God into our bedrooms, we are asking that He bless this time with one another. We are asking that He infuse us with the Holy Spirit so we can truly minister to each other's needs, desires, hurts, and wounds. Sex maybe the coming together of bodies. But holy intimacy is the coming together of souls. And anytime you spend time with the Lord, you always thank Him for showing up.

Expressing Love in All Seasons

When you reach your senior years, you can still enjoy intimacy by holding each other, kissing each other and just expressing love to each other. Don't stop expressing love because climax cannot be achieved.

Some women say their husbands are on medication and they no longer have a sexual desire. These women feel undesirable. Appeal to your husband if this is your situation. Say to him, "You may not be able to have an erection, but we can still enjoy intimacy. We may not get an orgasm, but we can still be intimate with each other. We can still bring each other pleasure, physically." This message has to be communicated between a husband and wife.

But, whatever you do to enjoy each other physically and spiritually, as well as emotionally, make sure you continue to be one with each other. Physical intimacy is a beautiful expression of the love between a husband and wife. Always remember to ask God to help you in this area and do it to

114

please Him. I promise you, God will sanctify you. He will anoint you to minister to your husband; He will anoint you to minister to your wife.

CHAPTER 9
The Marriage Covenant

"I take you to be my lawfully wedded husband/wife, to have and to hold from this day forward, for better, for worse; for richer or for poorer; in sickness and in health; to love and to cherish, until death do us part, according to God's holy ordinance."

Ah, the wedding vow. The words that are spoken in this eternal vow between a man and a woman were probably recorded in our psyches when we were children. We understood the words as a sign of the love that a husband and wife felt for each other. Those words were affirmed in the romantic novels we read as teens, or the romantic comedies we viewed as young adults. By the time we were the marrying age, we watched our friends and family members take the plunge and probably felt the "itch" to say these words to our future beloved.

I enjoy going to weddings and I especially get a kick out of watching those in attendance. Sometimes, couples sit closer together while the vows are exchanged. I often imagine they reflect on their own vows made years before. I catch glimpses of single women with a longing and hopeful look in their eyes. Most of them imagine themselves as the bride going to meet her "Prince Charming." For the most part, young single men pretend to be unaffected, but they too are hopeful that one day that special someone will come into their lives.

I can still remember the excitement I felt on the day of my daughter LaVette's wedding. Everyone was dressed in their formal outfits. Our family sat on the bride's side of the church, while my son-in-law's family and friends sat the groom's side of the church. The bridesmaids were dressed in burgundy gowns and groomsmen wore black tuxedoes. The minister waited at the front of the church with the Clarence, who was a very anxious groom. Finally the doors swung open and LaVette floated down the aisle on her father's arm. She was radiant, glowing and simply breathtaking and she walked to the front of the church to meet her beloved husband-to-be. Tears fell as they exchange their vows and the minister pronounces them man and wife.

Finally Clarence kissed LaVette and applause filled the sanctuary. This scene is that "happily ever after," or simply put, it is the fairytale of love.

I felt the same exhilarating enchantment almost 35 years ago when Vernon and I said our wedding vows. In my mind I just knew the love I had for him was enough. The ceremony was just that — a ceremony, because in my heart Vernon had been my husband long before the ceremony took place. We were both young. I was 17, Vernon was 18 and we were clueless about the vow that we had just made to one another and to God. It took having three children and becoming Christians for us to really understand the full obligation of the marriage vow.

Over the years, I have learned that when we take that vow, we are making the following commitment:

1. We choose to fully accept our mate as they are. We will not attempt to change them or to create them to be in the image of our liking.

2. We are saying that we are ready and willing to make the transition from son and daughter, boy and girl – to man and woman; husband and wife.

3. We will become "one flesh" and "leave our families and cleave to each other." The marriage must take on a life of it's own.

4. We are also vowing that we will delight and experience pleasure in our mate.

5. We promise to uplift our mate and help nurture their

gifts and talents as well as give them room to grow in the areas in which they are weak.

6. Finally, commit to unconditional love of our mate even in sickness, financial hardships, death of a parent, or and other hardships that life might bring.

7. We commit ourselves for the long haul and will not leave the marriage or our mates physically, spiritually, mentally or emotionally no matter the curve balls life throws our way.

Today, many couples view the marriage vow as nothing more than a legal contract. This is a mistake. When you enter into a covenant relationship it is based on love and trust whereas a contract is base on distrust and a way to protect the two parties of any unnecessary liabilities. A covenant, on the other hand, says regardless of the liabilities I am here with you. A contract says if one of the parties fails to live up to the others expectation. I have a legal escape hatch. I am no longer liable for what happens in the marriage. In covenant, there is unlimited responsibility on both parties within the marriage. In contract, there is a line that states what you will and will not be responsible for in the marriage.

For instance, a prenuptial agreement is drawn up to protect one's assets from the person they are marrying. This contract makes the marriage covenant null and void. You can't be in covenant and have a contract, too.

In God's eyes, a covenant is a binding agreement between two trusting parties who willingly agree to fulfill all obligations of the said agreement. It is a promise of the highest order. Covenant means an end to hatred, and an agreement to good service. It is the foundation of true friendship covered in unconditional love. The Bible says in Ecclesiastes 5:5 says: *it is better not to make a vow, then to make a vow and not pay.* Had we truly understood covenant, how God views covenants, I believe Vernon and I would have been more equipped to handle life's challenges. I also believe that had covenant been the foundation of our marriage from the onset, we would not have experienced the deadness in our relationship after the first five years.

God Is a Covenant Making God

Covenants are as old as time. God used them to tie us to Himself as a way to teach us the importance of keeping our word and the power our word has on people's lives.

The first covenant God made with us was with Adam and Eve in the Garden of Eden. (Gen. 3:21). The second covenant was with Noah. God decided to make a covenant with Noah by saving them from the impending flood. (Gen. 6:18).

The Lord fully establishes His covenant with man through Abraham. God tells Abraham that He will make his descendants more numerous than the stars (Gen. 15:5).

God made a covenant with Moses and the Children of Israel after He had delivered them from the hands of Pharaoh and the Egyptians (Exodus 19:5). God also made a covenant with David saying his house will establish his kingdom forever (2 Sam. 7:13-16).

The ultimate covenant God made with humanity in complete unconditional love was the shed blood of His son, Jesus – the descendant of David. Through Jesus Christ, we gain eternal life with our Heavenly Father. The covenants before Jesus were made with the blood of animals, but Jesus was the last and only living sacrifice that gives humanity permanent redemption from sin.

Roles in a Covenant Marriage

The Lord viewed covenants in biblical times as a very serious matter. He views the modern marriage covenant with the same intensity. When you choose to come together as husband and wife, you pledge yourselves to certain commitments. Those commitments include becoming "one flesh," meaning the marriage should reflect the union of the Holy Trinity. In that relationship, the Father, the Son, and the Holy Spirit each have different roles and distinct personalities yet they are one. *"The same nature and essence, equal members, intimate in relationship, and share a common purpose."*

In the same manner, the husband and wife are joined in the same way. They are "one flesh," but they have different roles to fulfill. It may be on the job, at church or maybe as a board member of an organization. Take me for instance. God anointed me to be an evangelist, but He also called me to be Vernon's wife and my children's mother. I have a special anointing as a speaker, but when I step off the platform, I step back into my role as my husband's wife, and my children's mother, which I believe are the greater callings in my life. I am able to evangelize *because* I am a wife and mother. Being in these roles allows me to witness how the power of God moves most in my life. These roles ground me, and enable me to minister to God's people. Because I understand that being a wife and mother is the foundation of my ministry, I keep my focus on my relationship with the Lord, and then on my relationships with my husband and children. In turn, the Lord blesses my ministry by continually feeding me revelations about His Word and how He wants it to free and heal His people.

My husband fills the role as priest, prophet, and king of the household. But how should he express that role and carry out that responsibility in partnership with me? The best example of a godly husband is Christ and his relationship with the church.

In Ephesians 5:25-29 it says, *"Husbands, love your*

wives, just as Christ also loved the church and gave Himself for her" Paul tells the Ephesians that the husband is to lead the family and be the head for the wife. He is to do so in humility,

Love, and sacrifice. Nowhere does the Scripture say that the husband should wield his authority over his wife in dominance and oppression. On the contrary, he is to treat her as his equal, which she is. He is to ask her opinions, listen to her heart, nurture her gifts and talents, provide for her and protect her always.

(1 Peter 3:7) say that *"Husbands, likewise, dwell with (your wives) with understanding, giving honor to the wife, as to the weaker vessel, and as being heirs together of the grace of life, that your prayers may not be hindered."* Peter tells husbands that they are to know their wives inside and out because she is his helpmate in life. She is his aide. And if he doesn't know her, meaning know her gifts and talents, her mind, and her heart, then he won't be able to tell her how she can effectively use her gifts and talents to help him fulfill the vision God gave him for the family. Peter reminds husbands to honor and cherish their wives in all that they do. They are not to take their wives for granted. He also lets husbands know that any time they refuse to make the above examples happen, her cries of disappointment, sorrow, and anger will block his prayers from God's ears. God will hear her cries above anything the husband is asking until he cares for her as he would his own body. Peter tells husbands to care for their wives as they would care for their own bodies for no man willingly abuses his own body.

When we talk about knowing each other, think of this as understanding your mate so well that you know just how they feel by the tone in their voice or a look in their eyes. You know their mood swings and why they act the way they do. You know when they're hiding the truth or trying to spare your feelings. You know when they give you their all or if they just doing something halfway. You know how much pressure to apply to inspire them, and you know when to back off.

I liken this to knowing your mate the way my husband knows cars. He can listen to the hum of an engine and tell you How many cylinders the car runs on. He can listen to the motor and tell what's wrong with it. As mates, it is critical that we dwell with one another according to knowledge and understanding. This is the only way a marriage is insured to thrive and go the distance. You must both be invested. It is crucial that you both take an active interest in the other person and see the importance of your personality differences as tools for your success.

Personality Differences Within A Covenant

My husband and I are very different, he is organized, and I am not. I tend to go with the flow, and he is very structured. He is very playful, and I am more serious. It took years for us to understand just how well the Lord had fit us together and balanced us.

At first we thought of each other as aliens. I didn't understand Vernon and he didn't understand me. We loved each other, but we didn't really know each other. For instance, for the longest time Vernon couldn't understand how God could use someone as unorganized as I am and work through me so powerfully in order to help free and heal thousands of people. By the same token, I had trouble understanding how God could use Vernon to give godly counsel to so many people, when he can be so distant and private. Yet, in the Spirit, these differences did not interfere with the purpose of God. In the natural, God still had to works things out with us.

Over the years, Vernon and I discovered that our differences gave us the opportunity to nurture one another's gifts and talents as well as help one another in weak areas of our lives. For example, I lose phone numbers. I make promises and forget that I even made them. Vernon comes behind me, picks up my notes and calls people to cover for me. He handles the situations as though he got the notes straight from me. As a result, I tease Vernon and tell him God has given him a phone ministry. Vernon makes these connections with people and ministers to them as if they were sitting right next to him. It's beautiful to watch, and it's interesting how God uses my weakness and makes it a strength for my husband.

By the same token Vernon loves his privacy and sometimes I have to very tactfully draw him out of his shell. Once he gets into the mix, trust me when I say that he can be the life of the social gathering.

Walking the Distance in Covenant

When a marriage reflects the union of the Holy Trinity, and couples can appreciate the differences each mate brings to the union and the relationship has a good chance of going the distance. In order to accomplish this end you must see your mate as your partner and not your competitor.

As a competitor, your whole goal is to out do your mate and squash him or her at every turn. Each person is out for "self." A victory for one is a defeat for the other. All experiences strengthen the individuals only; and the marital bond is no bond at all. The goal of competition is that in the end only one is left standing strong. For a marriage, this is a recipe for disaster.

Instead, think of your marriage as a long distance journey in which each of you desire to finish the course as partners instead of two competing individuals. As partners, you root for one another, you challenge one another, and you aid one another. Along the journey, each of you will reach personal goals of triumph. In those cases, your partner will celebrate with you because they would have been your personal cheerleaders while you struggled to reach that goal.

Your partner's personal victory in this case is a shared victory. On the opposite end, when tragedy strikes, the partners pull together. One partner's sadness or pain is empathized by the other. The burden is shared, and neither partner feels alone in their grief. In both scenarios, the partners' life experiences strengthen the marital bond and in the end, both stand strong. Becoming partners is one way to bolster the spirit of your marriage. Other ways include the following:

❖ Make a choice to love your mate unconditionally.
❖ Become fiercely loyal. Give your mate plenty of hugs affection.
❖ Don't give in to pride, bitterness and self-centeredness.
❖ Give each other room for failure.
❖ Be committed to quickly restoring harmony after conflict.
❖ Be quick to hear, but slow to speak and slow to anger. Be quick to forgive.
❖ Speak encouraging words to your mate on a daily basis.
❖ Avoid arguments created on purpose. Use a soft answer to put away wrath.
❖ When angry, don't say everything that you are thinking. Cool off first.
❖ Be committed to growing spiritually, mentally, emotionally, and physically.

But just as I've learned that these things bolster a marriage, I've also learned the major things that will tear a marriage down:

❖ Putting your own pleasure and interest before that of your mate.
❖ Wanting to have your way above God's will even if that means hurting your mate.
❖ Being so self-absorbed that you think everyone and everything revolves around you.
❖ Continually revisiting past offenses. Failing to forgive

❖ Refusing to be open to advice or correction from your mate.

❖ Placing people, work or any other interests above your mate.

❖ Being overly critical and insensitive.

The common thread among these areas that destroy the marriage is the "self." As we already understand, however, marriage isn't about the "self." It's about the partnership. That's what it means to be in covenant. God created humanity to walk in communion with one another — to walk in partnership. In Romans 12:9-10 it says, *"Let love be without hypocrisy. Abhor what is evil. Cling to what is good. Be kindly affectionate to one another with brotherly love, in honor giving preference to one another."*

In order for a covenant marriage to work it must done by always thinking of the other person. You're no longer a single man or woman. You are a husband or wife who now has a mate you've become accountable to and for.

As a way to demonstrate just what it means to be bound to someone and become "one flesh," some ministers perform the Salt Covenant during the marriage ceremony. Salt represents the power to strengthen food and keep it from decaying. It is a symbol of the pure truth of total surrender to the Lord in sacrificial love. As the minister explains this, a small bag of salt is given to each partner. The minister then tells each partner to take a pinch of their salt and put it into their partner's bag. Once the salt has been mixed, the bride and groom are told that if either can tell which grains of salt had belonged to their bag, that they are free to walk away from the marriage covenant. The truth of the matter is that you can't tell. The grains of salt all look alike. They taste alike. And their purpose is the same.

In marriage, you must consider yourselves one in the Spirit and one in the flesh. Though your roles will be different, and your personalities will vary, your purpose in life and the vision you share must be the same. That's what it means to be partners on a long distance journey.

Yours, Mine, and Ours in the Marriage Covenant

But how does covenant work in blended families where there is an ex-wife, an ex-husband, his children, your children and possibly grandchildren in the mix?

During a Valentine's Day conference in Alaska that was organized by my daughter LaVette, I realized that there were as many blended families as there were first-time couples. In listening to their concerns during the Question and Answer session, I realized they faced many challenges. I want to say that even though there may be extended people that come along with a marriage, the covenant is the same. The new wife or husband must understand that their new partner still has obligations to their former families. It is important to resolve any differences so that everyone involved can work together for the sake of the children and themselves. In (2 Sam. 21:7) David and Jonathan were in covenant where they became spiritual brothers. Years after Jonathan's deaths, David came into power and wanted to show a kindness to Jonathan's house. David searched high and low for a descendant of Jonathan. And when David found Mephibosheth, Jonathan's son, he honored him and took care of him out of respect for the covenant David made with Jonathan.

Security in Covenant

At the end of the day when everything is said and done, couples who commit themselves to living the marriage covenant will see and taste the fruit of their labor. Why? They will have learned to celebrate their differences, nurture one another's gifts, see life through their mate's eyes, and have made God the primary focus of their marriage. As rewards, they will rest in the awareness that God fulfills His promises as a covenant God.

There is security in knowing that our marriages are bound by covenant and that God honors covenants. Because God considers a covenant holy, our marriages are seen as holy promises. Not only do we have a vested interest in seeing our marriages through the journey, but God has a vested interest as well. This ensures that He will do everything in His power to help see us through to the end of the journey. God's desires to see us succeed, this should motivate us to approach Him with boldness, confidence, and great expectation. Remember God is on our side. He wants to see our marriages flourish. He wants to see our families endure. Nothing brings God more glory than to see families thrive.

"Therefore know that the Lord your God, He is God, the faithful God who keeps covenant and mercy for a thousand generations with those who love Him and keep His commandments," (Deut. 7:9).

CHAPTER 10
Winning Him Without a Word

I walked in the empty coffee shop, and found Mary in the smallest booth in the corner. We embraced. Her weary hug told me that my friend had passed the point of anger and slid into hurt. We sat across from each other. Mary's pink, puffy eyes stared deep into her untouched lukewarm coffee.

She let out a long and low sigh before speaking, "I can't take it anymore, Pat. The drinking, the parties, the flippant attitude toward my church friends and our Bible studies, the ordering me around instead of asking my opinion, his surprise dinner meetings at our house, and his kinky requests. I feel dirty all the time. I want out."

With that first utterance came more — the hurt, pain, disappointment, guilt and shame of loving a man who seemingly didn't love her tumbled from her lips in one long sentence. Mary shared her screaming escapes of trying to make him reason. She described how she would combat his negativity with Bible scriptures and quotes from her pastor. None ever worked. In fact, they fueled his rage all the more. It seemed like the more she stood her ground on wanting to do things God's way, the more her husband resisted her efforts to make him do right. Mary paused. I waited and let her thoughts mingle in the silence of the quiet coffee shop.

"Do you love him, Mary?" I asked.

"…yes…" she weakly answered.

"Do you want him?"

"Not like this…"

"Do you want him?" I asked with more strength in my voice.

"…I want my friend back."

I took her hand and she looked up. I spoke to Mary in my most gentle voice. "Then stop fighting him with words, and learn to win him with action instead."

Ministering to her that day was typical of the stories I had heard since coming into ministry and counseling in. Her story, like so many others, demonstrates the breakdown of a marriage when couples either stop fueling their relationship with God at the center, or one of them discovers God while the other balks at the changes taking place in their spouse. Those changes include not hanging out at old clubs or house parties; not enjoying the company of friends who drink, or smoke, or do drugs; wanting to go to church all the time, wanting to hold Bible studies in the home, wanting to attend events that are church-sponsored only, and wanting to be with other Christians. The rift always widens when the spouse who finds Jesus holds on to the Word for dear life just as the spouse who feels replaced and displaced holds on to their way of life without Jesus. Each partner fights the other out of sheer fear of losing what is dear to them hoping the other spouse will change their mind and come to reason.

The first mistake many women make in wanting to "change" their husbands' attitudes about Jesus is to share any and everything they've discovered in the Word as well as all of pastor's latest anecdotes and teachings. Ladies, we are not supposed to beat our husbands over their heads with the Word. We are not supposed to guilt them into believing in God. We are not supposed to throw ultimatums in their face to make them "do right." In addition, we are definitely not supposed to push what "pastor said" in our husbands' faces. However, we are supposed to win our husbands without a word.

Hurts, Heartaches, and Hindrances

First, please understand right now that your current marital state is not God's punishment for unconfessed sins, unforgiveness, rebellion, or disobedience. Sometimes God allows things to happen to fashion our character or the characters of the people around us. He knows exactly how much pressure it will take to shape us into the instrument He designed us to be in order to fulfill our purpose on this earth. Notice I said pressure. Your marital state is but a pressure to get the best out of you and out of your husband. *"We are hard-pressed on every side, yet not crushed; we are perplexed, but not in despair; persecuted, but not forsaken; struck down, but not destroyed—,"* (2 Cor. 4:8-9).

God wants the to get the glory out of our marriages. But He wants to know we will go the distance and not give up on ourselves or on Him. He wants to know we will be faithful to Him in any circumstance. Will we still call on Him? Will we still trust Him? Will we keep our faces toward Him? Or will we turn our backs on God and curse His name? Hear me when I say it is imperative at this juncture to ask God into your situation. *"Ask, and it will be given to you; seek, and you will find; knock, and it will be opened to you. For everyone who asks receives, and he who seeks finds, and to him who knocks it will be opened,"* (Matt. 7:7-8). God wants to be asked to come into your situation and create a miracle. But He will not come unless He is asked to come. It cannot happen unless you believe He is able to make it manifest. God works in the midst of our faith. *"Now faith is the substance of things hoped for, the evidence of things not seen,"* (Heb. 11:1). Without faith, there are no miracles. Without faith, there is no healing.

Because you and your husband on are on different paths, you will have to accept total responsibility for your own growth in the Lord. You will have to encourage yourself by yourself. Continue going to church, but don't bring church home unless your husband specifically asks you about service. When he asks, give a brief answer. Too much elaboration may backfire on you. He may throw salt on your joy by suddenly becoming disinterested in what you have to say. He may give an off-handed comment to spin you into an argument. This is not what you want. In chapter 5, we learned how harmony and unity diffuse drama. Keep this in mind as you try to win your husband without a word. If the situation begins to escalate, remember the Word says, *"a soft answer turns away wrath, but a harsh word stirs up anger. The tongue of the wise uses knowledge rightly, but the mouth of the fool pours forth foolishness,"* (Prov. 15:1-2). Don't follow your husband into the argument. Instead, back out of the argument without dishonoring or disrespecting him. These hindrances will test how you balance between honoring and respecting him, and growing spiritually and obeying God.

Understand Where You Are

To win our husbands to God, we must understand our current situations. Many of us are not married to born-again Christians. We got in this situation because:

❖ Both partners were unsaved when they got married, but afterward the woman accepts Christ and her husband does not.

❖ She thinks he is a believer before they married only to discover he was just religious.

❖ Both were ignorant to the fact that the marriage was not God's will.

❖ Or, you are a born-again Christian while your husband is a carnal Christian.

❖ In any case, you are now yoked with an unbeliever.

To be *yoked* means to be tethered or bound to someone who is your co-laborer in life. Ideally, you should be *yoked* with someone who is your equal in soul and spirit. You want to be with someone who shares the necessary core values, morals, and ethics that will allow both of you to grow spiritually, mentally, and emotionally together. In a covenant marriage, you strive to have your relationship reflect the harmony and unity of the Holy Trinity.

In biblical times, farmers yoked two oxen together to

131

plow a straight furrow in the field. The yoke binding the animals together would have been a bar made of wood or iron, depending on what had to be accomplished. By having two animals, alike in weight, height, strength, and kind, it was assured that the work would be done correctly. Oftentimes, the animals would have done the same type of labor previously, so that when they were yoked together, they would not be *confused* as to what they are being yoked to do. Scriptures says, " *Can two walk together, unless they are agreed?"* (Amos 3:3). In the above examples, labor and marriage have a better chance of working well when two equal partners walk as one.

To be *unequally yoked* is just the opposite. In fact, to be unequally yoked means that as a believer, you carry the spiritual, emotional, and physical load for two people because your spouse is spiritually dead. If equally yoked means two oxen can plow a field with straight rows, then being unequally yoked means an ox and an ass yoked together create crooked furrows and unplowed land. In the second example, the labor was for nothing, the land was ruined, and the animals were spent without yielding a good day's work.

Marriage done in an *unequally yoked* partnership is like the unequally yoked animals trying to plow a field. The labor is frustrating and infuriating, the marriage is strained, and the individuals in the partnership walk away wishing they could reclaim the time spent being miserable.

Scripture warns us: *"Do not be unequally yoked together with unbelievers. For what fellowship has righteousness with lawlessness? And what communion has light with darkness?"* (2nd Cor. 6:14). Here, God uses three key words to stress the areas that make it impossible for a believer and an unbeliever to be yoked together: fellowship, righteousness, and communion.

Fellowship is to enjoy those things the both of you have

in common, as well as share in the labor the two of you will do together in this life. Once you accepted Christ, your life appetites changed. You want to do more and more for God and less and less for the world. When you are yoked with someone who is spiritually dead, you cannot fellowship in the things that delight the Lord because the unbeliever doesn't understand why it's important to do so. They can't connect with you in that area of your life. And guess what? Once you have given your life to Christ, all areas of your life are His; you've been made new in the spirit. *"Therefore, if anyone is in Christ, he is a new creation; old things have passed away; behold, all things have become new,"* (2 Cor. 5:17).

Righteousness, according to Strong's Concordance, means just or being right or conforming your life so it resembles the revealed will of God. When you are a believer, it is your desire to live a life that is righteous before God and man. Now that you are a new creation in Christ, you understand *"He made Him who knew no sin to be sin for us, that we might become the righteousness of God in Him,"* (2 Cor. 5:21). If you are the righteousness of God, you look first to do God's work in this life. Your life focus is on how to please God, how to do God's will, and how to live a life that fulfills the mission God implanted in your spirit before the beginning of time. All else becomes secondary.

Unbelievers are just the opposite. Their first allegiance is to themselves and to the world. They don't obey or trust God. Instead, they rebel against God and do what seems right to them — hoping for the best. They follow the ways of the world, and hunger and thirst after the world.

Communion, or to be in union with, means to be bound in partnership and fellowship where there is a mutual and open sharing of experiences and of the self. When you are a child of the Light, you know God dwells within you. You know you are to share your light with others. Light breaks the darkness. In the beginning, God separated the light from the dark. Before you admitted Him into your life, you walked in darkness. Light and darkness cannot coexist in the same space. Scripture says, *"God is light and in Him is no darkness at all,"* (1 John 1:5b). If you walk with God, you cannot walk in darkness.

Unbelievers are dead to the things of God and walk blindly in life. They stumble trying to make sense of their existence only to realize there is no sense in the world's chaos. Only God brings order, light, and purpose. Because they have turned their backs on God, or never opened their hearts to Him, they wander aimlessly in life never fulfilling their purpose nor experiencing true and everlasting peace. God warns us of this in 1 John 1:15-17:

"Do not love the world or the things in the world. If anyone loves the world, the love of the Father is not in him. For all that is in the world — the lust of the flesh, the lust of the eyes, and the pride of life — is not of the Father but is of the world. And the world is passing away, and the lust of it; but he who does the will of God abides forever."\

In an unequally yoked marriage, the saved spouse realizes how much she has to cling to the things of God in order to coexist with her spouse in some semblance of harmony. She cannot look to her partner for a complete union because it won't happen. Instead, she must change her focus. She must look to God to fulfill the areas of her life left void because of the unsaved spouse. However, all is not lost. Hear me when I say harmony is possible. Unity on some level is possible. But what is not possible is complete harmony and complete unity. So stop looking for it. It will not come until your spouse gives his life to Christ.

However, I promise you when you change your focus to God, God will change your marriage. He did it for me and I know He will do it for you. When you pull your focus toward God, He will then strengthen you to do the work needing to be done in you and in your marriage.

I started this chapter saying we are to win our husbands without a word. Knowing where you are in your marriage and changing the focus from your husband to God is the first step. The next step is to understand what is at stake in your marriage.

Understand Your Fight of Faith

In a marriage where both partners are saved, you can fight the good fight of faith together. You both understand the world doesn't want your marriage to last and will do everything it can to tear it asunder. You understand what it means to be in a spiritual battle and you can go to God pleading for Him to step into your situation.

In a marriage where only the wife is saved, the fight is different. Not only do you fight to keep your marriage and your family spiritually covered, but also you fight to win your husband to God. Satan doesn't mind if only the wife is saved because he understands family order. The husband has headship over the family, just as Christ has headship over the Church. If the headship is not submitted to God, then Satan can get a foothold in the marriage and destroy it. Satan doesn't want the Church to thrive. Satan doesn't want Christ to come back for His bride. Get this in your spirits. Your battle is not against your husband. *"For we do not wrestle against flesh and blood, but against principalities, against powers, against the rulers of the darkness of this age, against spiritual hosts of wickedness in the heavenly places,"* (Eph. 6:12).

The enemy tells lies about our marital situations. To women who are married to unsaved men, the enemy whispers: "Honey, if only your husband would give his life to the Lord then you could have devotions together, read the Word of God together, and pray together. You wouldn't be a church widow. He'd come to church with you and you would have marital bliss." Lie! Those of us who are married to saved men know we may experience a level of fulfillment, but the grass isn't greener on our sides. We have our own challenges that include:

- ❖ "He will never become the man that God has designed him to become."
- ❖ "He will always be insensitive toward you and he will never understand you."
- ❖ "No other man in the church has the struggles or weaknesses he has."
- ❖ "You will never be a priority in his life."
- ❖ "If you submit to him, he will control you."
- ❖ "He will never share his true and honest feelings with you."
- ❖ Satan has a way of using your needs and fears to send you tormenting messages, keeping you from trusting God to work on your behalf.

The enemy fills our heads with these lies to keep us confused about the fight on our hands. Absolute words like "always and never" are designed to make us feel trapped or fighting a battle that has no way of ever ending or being resolved. These lies feed on our fears and tear apart our self-esteem to the point where trusting God is impossible.

Trust me when I say the lies are a setup to keep our marriages in bondage. The lies force us to believe our marriages would be easy if our husbands submitted to God. As long as we stay confused, our marriages will stay under attack. The longer our marriages stay under attack, the easier it is for the enemy to destroy our families and our lives. For the Scriptures say, *"Be sober, be vigilant; because your adversary the devil walks about like a roaring lion, seeking whom he may devour,"* (1 Peter 5:8).

Ladies, it's time to roll up your sleeves and get to work. The Word says, when we are about to do battle, we must put on the whole armor of God. The armor equips us to withstand life's challenges so that in the end, we realize we did all we could to stand. When you took your marriage vow, it said for better or for worse. You vowed to be in the marriage completely — heart, mind, body, and soul. Fighting for your husband's salvation is part of this package deal. There is no out. Being married doesn't guarantee you will always be comfortable. Being married doesn't guarantee you will never cry, be disappointed, hurt, or lonely, it just means you hope the person in your life shares your life. That's all. Now is not the time to give up. Now is the time to dig in.

Paul addressed this situation in his first letter to the Corinthians. He said, *"If any brother has a wife who does not believe, and she is willing to live with him, let him not divorce her. And a woman who has a husband who does not believe, if he is willing to live with her, let her not divorce him. For the unbelieving husband is sanctified by the wife; and the unbelieving wife is sanctified by the husband,"* (1st Cor. 7:13-14). Paul's response was to ensure the couples their marriages were still valid and real. One would not have to divorce his or her spouse because they decided to follow Christ. On the contrary, Paul encouraged them to stay together because the influence of the spouse who followed Christ on the unbeliever could win that spouse to Christ.

Paul also knew the only way for the church in Corinth to stay alive and grow was to keep marriages intact. The quickest way to destroy a church is to destroy families and couples.

The key elements to protect marriage are prayer, affirmation, communication, honor, respect, apologies, forgiveness, and trust in God. These tools are not meant only for the household where both partners are saved. These tools are meant for households where only one partner is saved and is the spiritual covering for the entire family.

Some of you may be in a critical place in your marriage because you have to make a choice. Is your marriage worth saving? When you look at the pros and cons of what is in front of you, you must be brutally honest with yourself. If you find he is a good man who loves you, wants only the best for you, treats you like gold, provides for you, protects you, loves your children, and doesn't stand in your way to loving God — then work with your man. Know that God loves him and wants him to experience everlasting peace in the kingdom.

Your fight will be to understand that your labor may have no immediate rewards. Earlier I explained that once Vernon got on board with God, he was able to reciprocate my love for him. In the fight for your husband's salvation, there may be no reciprocation — at least not readily and definitely not in the spirit. But, know that God will not forget you. Your sacrifice will not go unrewarded. The muscles you gain from this sacrifice will be the fruit of the Spirit: "...*love, joy, peace, longsuffering, kindness, goodness, faithfulness, gentleness (and) self control,*" (Gal. 5:22). The first three fruits describe your relationship with God. The second three describe your relationships with others, i.e. your husband. The last three describe the conduct with which you must carry yourself as a believer.

I know this is a lot to take in. Believe me, when I went through my own marital wilderness journey, no one could have prepared me for the confusing and conflicting emotions that bombarded me. There were days I loved my husband. There were days that I wished he would disappear. But, I am glad I hung in there and didn't let go.

If you decide your marriage is worth fighting for, here are some tools you can use to win your husband without a word.

138

Win Him Without a Word

OK! This is it. We have rolled up our collective sleeves and decided our marriages are worth the fight. Now we need to understand how to fight the good fight of faith. In 1 Peter 3:1-4 we are instructed on how to do this: *"Wives, likewise, be submissive to your own husbands, that even if some do not obey the word, they, without a word, may be won by the conduct of their wives, when they observe your chaste conduct accompanied by fear. Do not let your adornment be merely outward — arranging the hair, wearing gold, or putting on fine apparel — rather let it be the hidden person of the heart, with the incorruptible beauty of a gentle and quiet spirit, which is very precious in the sight of God."*

In this passage, Peter lists five things you must do to win your husband: submit to him, live a chaste life, fear the Lord, dress modestly, and develop a heart that exhibits a gentle, quiet and reverent spirit. In addition to this, you must learn to do these things as a service to God with your husband as the beneficiary. Winning your husband without a word means serving him because you love God. If you notice, we have discussed all of these key elements in the entire book. Which means, everything you've learned thus far in dealing with a saved husband applies to your unsaved husband.

Key element number one: submission. Even though your husband is not submitted to God just yet, does not mean you don't submit to him. You do because you married him and you promised God you would aid him. Not only did you promise God you would aid him, but you made a "covenant vow" to live your life as a couple. Now, you must follow through.

Submitting to your husband shows you trust him. Men need to feel trusted. They need to feel their word, presence, and counsel mean something to you. Submitting to them means fueling their dreams. Nothing touches a man more than a woman who believes in his dream. When you do things to aid the dream, you draw him closer to you. The closer you draw him to you, the closer you draw him to God.

Your trust and faith in him must be sincere. Men can smell fakeness a mile away. As long as you focus on pleasing and trusting God, submitting to your husband will become easier. The easier you submit to him, the more he will begin to trust you. Do not take his trust for granted because there is no guarantee you'll get it back if you lose it. When men begin to trust us, they soar. They do things they never thought they could do. They accomplish their dreams faster. Their goals become crystal clear. They trust you with their secrets. And, they let down their emotional guards. A woman who allows a man to be himself in every aspect of himself is rare indeed. Scripture even says this quality is something a virtuous woman should have: *"The heart of her husband safely trusts her; So he will have no lack of gain,"* (Prov. 31:11).

Key element number two: live a chaste life. To be chaste means to be "pure". Pure, or hagnos in Greek, means to be holy. Being pure means a thing is clean, modest, undefiled, morally faultless, and without blemish. How a woman behaves on a day-to-day basis can speak volumes to her husband. When her behavior lines up with the things of God, her compassion level is high, but her tolerance for hate is low to nothing. Her moral character is flawless and her reputation is solid. A woman who lives a chaste life will hear her children and husband bless her name. Scripture agrees: *"Her children rise up and call her blessed; Her husband also and he praises her: 'Many daughters have done well, But you excel them all,'"* (Prov. 31:28-29). Not only will they sing her praises but her reputation in the neighborhood will be solid as well, and her husband's name will be synonymous with excellence. Her chase behavior allows her husband to clearly see the jewel he really married.

Key element number three: fear the Lord. Scripture says, *"The fear of the Lord is the beginning of wisdom,"* (Psalm 111:10). To fear God means to know Him — to know His qualities, His character, His thoughts, and His feelings. To reach this level of intimacy, you must have a relationship with God such that His qualities, character, thoughts, and feelings will be first-hand knowledge. A woman who is this intimate with the Lord not only fears Him and His awesome power, but is humbled by His grace and favor.

In addition to knowing who God is, she is a woman who exhibits great wisdom. To obtain godly wisdom one must follow in the footsteps of the Lord by keeping His laws and sitting at His feet. People over the centuries have traveled great lengths to obtain such wisdom. Queen of Sheba traveled over the scorching desert to sit at the feet of King Solomon. Mary, the sister of Martha, sat at Jesus' feet listening to His teachings and became one of his first women disciples. Both the Queen of Sheba and Mary understood that *"the fear of the Lord is the **instruction** of wisdom, And before honor is humility,"* (Prov. 15:33).

Key element number four: dress modestly. Ladies, we discussed that men are visual creatures. This Scripture says our adornment should not be "merely" of the outside appearance. Just because we are now serving our husbands as we would serve the Lord doesn't mean we shouldn't hook ourselves up. Earlier, I mentioned how a woman's countenance says a lot about the man in her life. Now that you've changed your focus, your "man" is God. God still wants us to look good because it tells the world He is a good provider, a protector, and is definitely a lover of our souls. God makes us happy and brings us pleasure; therefore, we serve God in gladness and joy.

To keep you on target with how God wants you to look, when you get dressed in the morning ask yourself the following questions: Is the outfit too revealing? Does it flatter my frame, or is the outfit wearing me? Does my makeup enhance my natural beauty? Is my hair in an up-to-date style? Do I smell good or is the cologne a little too strong? Are my teeth pearly white and my breath fresh, or is it past time to go to the dentist? Does my skin glow with health or has ash and acne taken over?

It's perfectly fine to look your best. After all, Proverbs 31:22 says, *"Her clothing is fine linen and purple."* Here, the virtuous woman dresses well and like royalty. Looking good is a good thing. However, you don't want to dress as if you have no husband. Being married means you are set apart. You don't dress to attract attention to yourself — especially of the opposite sex. To do so would add undo stress and drama in your household, and shame and disappointment to your husband. Men like to see their wives dressed well, but it crushes them to see their wives dressed too provocatively. As the wife, your job is to promote peace, unity, and harmony in the marriage. Dress for God first, your husband second, and you third.

Key element number five: develop a quiet, reverent, and servant's spirit. As women, we serve outside the home in innumerable ways. But this means nothing if we aren't tending to our first ministry — our husbands. When we die, we will have to give an account of how we lived, which includes how we served and treated the people the Lord put in our care. In giving an account of ourselves to God, we must call to mind all of our actions done or not done during our time on earth (Romans 14:12). Because we are to be an ezer to our husbands, God will hold us accountable for how we serve or wait on our husbands. We are not to withhold help or godly counsel. Wise women influence the home, but when wives withhold their influence out of spite, bitterness, anger, rage, disappointment, confusion, or depression, the vision God has for the family and marriage cannot manifest. However, when you die to yourself and serve with a quiet and reverent spirit, you open the door for God's blessings to flow into your home and breathe life into your marriage and your family.

These five key elements: will help you maneuver in your marriages while God works to heal the broken spaces in your life and in the life of your spouse. As you are putting these things into practice, realize there may be some resistance from your spouse because the change you are trying to implement is counter to the world's culture. You are learning to live by God's laws, while your husband lives by the world's laws. These two points of view will often collide. However, how you handle those situations may mean the difference between saving your marriage and abandoning it.

Know When Enough Is Enough

There is a point when doing all you can to win him without a word leaves the realm of gentle nudging met with annoying resistance, and enters the land of irreconcilable discord and abuse. Mental, emotional, physical, sexual, and spiritual abuse should never be tolerated. Ever. Because the more you tolerate the subtle abuse, the more you are desensitized to how your spirit and self-esteem are being chipped away on a daily basis. The more you are desensitized, the easier it will be to slide into physical abuse.

There are always warning signs. Some of those signs include:

- ❖ He makes all the decisions without your input
- ❖ He controls everything about you (from hair length and color to clothes and make-up)
- ❖ He picks your friends
- ❖ People around you with positive or negative influence threaten him
- ❖ He urges you to disconnect from family, even if the relationships are healthy

143

❖ He always chooses your meals in restaurants and is upset if you persist on making your own choices
❖ Being with him forces you to question every decision you're use to making on your own

It is our job to know the signs and be able to pinpoint them when they show up in our relationships. Do not dismiss those things that hurt your feelings or are said in an off-handed way. I don't care how charming he is, or how much money he spends on you and your children. Snide remarks hidden by "just joking" are yellow flags trying to warn you of a problem. The more the yellow flags show up, the more you need to take a step back and really get a good look at your situation — no matter how long you've been married or how short you've been dating.

In a dating situation, if you feel dishonored and disrespected, it would be wise to confront it and or end the relationship, immediately, and permanently. You don't need this. No matter what has happened in your life, there is nothing that justifies this treatment. God can send a man who knows how to treat you with respect and honor. You don't have to "work" with what is in front of you, especially if what is in front of you is truly "a piece of work." Life is too short and God's assignment for our lives is too urgent to put up with foolishness, which could end in your death. It is better to be alone and alive, than to be dating and end in a coffin.

In a marriage situation, understand there is no special reward in heaven waiting for you for staying in a physically or mentally abusive marriage. God did not create us to be abused, and He receives no glory from this situation. *"So then, my beloved brethren, let every man be swift to hear, slow to speak, slow to wrath; for the wrath of man does not produce the righteousness of God,"* (James 1:19-20). Staying in a physically abusive situation is poor stewardship of your bodies.

If you are in this situation, I advise you to get to safety. Do not confuse submission with being oppressed. There is a difference. We voluntarily submit to our husbands because we submit to God. In this situation, trust is a key factor. Being oppressed means violating someone else's will. God did not create women to be treated as doormats by anyone.

Over the years, I have counseled couples and women who have found themselves in situations where they had to decide whether the relationship was worth salvaging. If we were experiencing mental, emotional and spiritual abuse, my advice was to nip it in the bud. Do not tolerate the verbal digs. Do not tolerate the mind games. Do not tolerate the "holier than thou" attitudes. Do not accept guilt trips. All of this leads to anger and resentment. The more you tolerate this behavior, the more hate and unforgiveness build up in your spirit against your spouse. Then, one day you will look up and wonder why you have an urge to do away with him or her. Anger kills — literally and figuratively.

Do not tolerate these things. Immediately confront your spouse. Tell him or her that the behavior is intolerable. Offer your spouse a book, tape, or a CD. Suggest that the two of you go to a marriage conference where you will receive godly teaching about marriage as well as be surrounded by other couples in similar situations. At this stage, the idea is to work out the problem one on one. You can tell your spouse how the behavior makes you feel and how it demoralizes you. Let your spouse know that the behavior tears at the root of your being and hinders you from being your best self.

If your spouse refuse to listen, acknowledge the problem, or refuse to go to a marriage conference, let your spouse know you are bringing in a third party to help you work through your issues. The third party can be a parent, minister, or friend whom both of you trust, respect and know will give you godly counsel. This person must be someone who is for your marriage and wants to see you stay together. By bringing in a third party, you tell your spouse that you are seriously concerned about your marital health and about not allowing the abuse to go unnoticed. In this setting, both of you will become accountable to your counselor and must take the advice given if salvaging the marriage is what you are committed to do.

Abuse is wrong no matter if it comes from the husband or the wife. Over the years, I have counseled a number of men married to abusive women. My advice to them has been the same as my advice to women. So readers, if you find yourselves in an abusive situation use the above process. If you are married to someone who wants to honor the marriage covenant and remain married, then he or she will find a way to change their behavior once it is brought to their attention.

Marriage Is a Walk of Faith

Know that God wants what's best for us in the midst of our situations. In His larger plan for the world, God needs whole and healthy people to build His church upon. Bleeding marriages bring God no glory. This is why we must surrender our marriages and our husbands to the Lord. When we place our marriages on God's altar, we believe He will honor our covenants. This step toward God allows Him to fill us with complete grace and mercy. He hears our hearts cry out to him about our marriages and sees the tears drench our pillows. These things move Him to encourage us to hold on and trust Him. *"Trust in the Lord with all your heart, And lean not on your own understanding; In all your ways acknowledge Him, And He shall direct your paths,"* (Prov. 3:5-6).

Know that God has a plan for our marriages. To know His plan is to be immersed in His Word, for in it is the instruction for healthy and holy living. As you digest the Word, you will be more equipped to handle the obstacles your marriage presents on a daily basis, and your walk with the Lord will be closer and more intimate than you could imagine. Before you know it, you and your spouse will have walked 30, 40, or 50 years as a covenant couple who learned through the seasons of marriage how to endure the decades.

CHAPTER 11
Seasons of Marriage

In 1998, Vernon promised me that when he turned 50 in 2000 he would completely retire and help me in ministry. When 2000 rolled around, he wasn't ready. He felt there were things he still wanted to put together financially before totally letting go. I said OK and never said another thing about it. Two years later, he came to me out of the blue and said he was ready. We went to our favorite spot in the mountains and spent time with the Lord asking that God would give Vernon peace about this move and that God would bless us in this new venture. When we left, Vernon was at complete peace.

Years ago, when Vernon said he wanted to stay in the military, it took everything within me to say OK. With him now telling me that he was ready to retire altogether and join me in ministry, I understood that we had come full circle. My partner in life is now my co-labor for Christ, and nothing pleases me more. As we travels together, it is a blessing to know that he is with me to cover me and to be a support in the work God has called us to.

Looking back over my year with Vernon, I mark our growth as a couple and as individuals by the character building experiences he and I have gone through together. Each challenge we experienced as parents, as a couple, or as individuals trying to live out our purpose, became a season in our marriage that forced us to grow stronger, wiser, and better equipped to handle what life would throw our way. I liken these seasons to the marriage vows: "for better or for worse," "for richer or for poorer," and "in sickness and in health." These six seasons broke us down, and built us back up. They chiseled away selfishness and pride, and nurtured selflessness and humility. They taught us the power of forgiveness and the necessity of active communication. These six reoccurring seasons always stripped us of a self-centered quality only to replace it with a God-centered one.

Every couple will eventually go through these seasons. God designed these seasons to toughen and strengthen marriages so they will endure the decades. When God put couples together, He did it so their life journey would not be lonely and the work He purposed for each of us would be accomplished through teamwork. But guess what? True teamwork is only perfect in the midst of challenges that need to be overcome. The best way for couples to hone their teamwork skills is to go through the seasons.

For Better or For Worse

The years we traveled all over the world while Vernon was in active duty was our "for better or for worse" season. It was a time when we learned how to be flexible, less controlling, patient, open-minded, and very sensitive to each other's needs. We learned to view the time we spent as a family and as a couple as a priority. Traveling stretched and matured us. We developed skills that complemented each other and allowed the family to grow from a stable foundation.

But all "for better or for worse" seasons aren't as neat. Sometimes, you find yourself fighting to keep your marriage while your spouse desperately fights to leave because of shame, guilt, or feelings of unworthiness.

That's what happened to John and Mary (I've changed their names to protect their privacy). I met John several years ago on my way to Pensacola, Fla. to speak at a singles conference. He was on my connection flight into Dallas, Texas. At this time, it had been a while since I spoke to singles and I wanted to take advantage of the time I had on my flight to go over my notes. I took my seat by the window. For a while, no one sat in my row. "Good," I thought. "I'll be able to use the middle seat to spread out my materials and be comfortable." No sooner had I expressed those sentiments than a young man sat down in the isle seat. As we exchanged pleasantries, we gave each other a look that said neither one of us wanted to be chatty.

I opened my notes and pulled out my Miles Monroe book entitled, *"Single, Married, Separated, and Divorced."* John glanced over at me. When his eye landed on the book title, his whole face lit up with hope.

"Is that book any good?" he asked.

"I haven't read it, but I trust the author. He's an excellent teacher. I've read a few of his other books and enjoyed them," I said, waiting.

"…You think the book will work?" he asked with a hint of sadness.

"Yes, I believe it will," I assured him.

John paused for a moment, then said, "I need help. My wife called me last night and said she was leaving me. The guilt of her past affair is too much to live with. She wants out."

His voice shook. It was obvious he had no idea she felt this way or that their marriage was even in crisis. He was to meet his wife in Dallas and didn't know how to respond to her in light of this news. After listening to him, I asked him three questions.

"John, do you love your wife? Do you want your marriage? Are you ready to please God? If you can answer yes to any one of these questions then it is possible to rebuild your marriage with your wife."

I shared my testimony and my belief that God would fill John with all power to help him go through this "for better or for worse" season. God honors those who honor their covenant marriage. If John still loved his wife, God would help

150

him learn how to understand her pain, confusion, anger, disappointment, and guilt. God would show John how to meet his wife where she is and walk with her through this. If John didn't know if he loved her, but knew he loved God, God would honor His relationship with John. God would fill John with His agape love thereby healing John's heart and pouring out an abundance of grace upon him and his relationship with his wife. If John wanted to walk away from everything, yet he loved God and wanted to continue to grow in his relationship with Him, God would give John the strength to do what was necessary to respond godly to his painful and broken relationship.

John thought about everything and was able to answer yes to all three questions. For the rest of the trip, we talked about the mistakes he made being a workaholic and totally neglecting the emotional needs of his wife and family. When we landed in Dallas, John and I had prayed and exchanged numbers. I promised him that Vernon and I would keep John and his wife in our prayers.

Shortly after I returned home, I spoke with Mary. A little later on in the month, Vernon spoke with her and John. We continued this phone ministry over the next year. I didn't meet Mary until a year after our initial phone conversation while speaking at a conference in Dallas. She was such a pleasant person and worth the fight. Periodically over the next 2 or 3 years, Mary and I talked. I never spoke with John on the phone again.

That was in 1996. Recently while in Dallas visiting my sister Carolyn and her family, her pastor introduced me to the congregation. Though I had been at the church for its women's retreat, the pastor wanted the entire congregation to meet me. To my surprise, John and Mary walked up to me holding hands and smiling. They were still together. God had changed their "worse" situation into a "better" and stronger marriage.

151

The season of "for better or for worse" tests the resolve of every couple. Each test builds endurance muscles, which is what is needed to be and stay married. No one stays married 30, 40, or 50 plus years off love alone. It takes the patience, endurance, and trust learned during this season to create a marital foundation that can't be rocked to the ground. Much of what I learned in this season gave me the building blocks necessary to fight for my marriage.

For Richer or For Poorer

Once you choose to live for Christ, your whole outlook on life changes. The things that used to be important to you aren't important anymore. As Vernon and I continued to study the Word, we developed a deep desire to experience the true riches God has to offer each believer. To gain those true riches is spelled out in Proverbs 22:4, *"By humility and the fear of the Lord Are riches and honor and life."* Here, we see that to obey God's commands, nurture a relationship with Him, and serve His people in a spirit of humility ushers in riches, honor, and life. Vernon and I later discovered what kind of life God wants for every believer. Jesus spells it out in John 10:10, *"I have come that they (believers) may have life, and that they may have it more abundantly."* Abundance means more than enough, overflowing, surplus, extraordinary, and excessive. Imagine that: an excessive life. Sounds rich to me!

So Vernon and I choose to live life by walking in the Spirit, which meant developing an intimate relationship with God. To nurture such a relationship, Vernon and I made sure our home would be a home of peace, or a Shalom House. No matter what country or city we lived, our home was always known as a place of rest. It was where we worshipped, prayed, studied the Word, and led many people to Christ. This was truly a rich season in our lives. We were able to minister to the wounded and broken, and see immense healing take place. I can remember neighbors saying, "Girl, I just needed to rest." I would leave the room to offer them some type of sandwich or drink of water only to come back to find them asleep on my couch. My children would come home from school or play and find our couch occupied. I would explain to them sometimes God removes us from a hectic environment to one of peace so He can re-energize our spirits. The children would understand and adjust their behavior to not disturb the atmosphere of peace and healing that had been created.

Though we experienced the richness of an intimate relationship with God, Vernon and I never really experienced a season of being "well off" financially as the children were growing up. I remember one time in the Netherlands around 1981 we had an opportunity to purchase a Volvo at an incredible price. We've always had good credit and believed getting the car should be a breeze. We applied for credit and were denied. Stunned, Vernon and I went home and prayed. The very next morning during my devotion time with the Lord, I read the story in Exodus 16 and Numbers 11 about the Israelites not being satisfied with manna and God granting them what they wanted but with it He sent leanness to their souls. I shared this with Vernon, and he decided not to press the car issue. Please understand there is nothing wrong with material things. But when material things cool our affections toward God, we need to re-examine our motives for wanting the thing in the first place. Vernon and I preferred to develop a rich relationship with the Lord and didn't mind sacrificing financial gain for it.

Another of our sacrifices was a loss of a second income: mine. When the children were small, I wanted to be at home with them. I have always wanted to raise my own children. I never wanted to leave them with a sitter. Because we were always moving, it was hard finding a sitter we could trust. So becoming a stay-at-home mom was an easy choice. I convinced Vernon I could save him money by staying at home. I even calculated how much money I could save. I added up the cost of potential daycare, new work clothes for me, gas money, lunch money, etc. He quickly agreed. I promised him I would sacrifice my weekly shopping sprees. No charge card usage. Nothing extra! I would be satisfied with his income alone.

This season of poorer put the lesson of leaving and cleaving to the test. Could I really be satisfied with Vernon's income in order to be a stay-at-home mom? Because I am a woman of my word, I tightened the family's spending belt and learned how to stretch five cents to make five dollars. We took the kids to the beach with packed lunches. Vernon made fabulous popcorn that we ate while watching TV. Instead of going to the movies, the kids stretched their imaginations with family talent shows. I took a class in cake decorating and baked the kids' birthday cakes. We went to the zoo and museums. I became coupon savvy and made clipping coupons a game for LaVette and I to enjoy. Every time I saved money honoring my promise to Vernon, I praised God.

During our "for richer or for poorer" season, Vernon and I learned the value of keeping God at the center of our lives. Our times of prayer, praise, and worship were always filled with a seasonal word from the Lord. I watched the children become stronger than siblings — they became friends. We learned to trust God to be our provider. In doing so, He supplied all our need according to His riches in glory by Christ Jesus, (Phil. 4:19).

In Sickness and in Health

Of all the seasons Vernon and I have gone through together, my season battling and overcoming Lupus between

1988 and 1991 was the greatest demonstration of what it means to honor a marriage covenant. This season is where every lesson discussed in this book is put to the test. You find yourself asking the following questions:

- ❖ Do I have the strength and the patience to nurture my spouse through this illness?
- ❖ Do I have the fortitude to be mother and father to our children?
- ❖ Am I willing to sacrifice time, money, and life to see my spouse well again?
- ❖ Can I believe for the both of us that death doesn't have to be the ultimate outcome?
- ❖ If death is inevitable, can I love my spouse to the very end with no regrets and not blame God in the process?

When exchanging this vow, we don't expect to face this season until old age. We understand that no one lives forever. But, you don't figure that forever will come at age 36. That's how old I was when Lupus knocked on my door and decided to stay awhile.

After marrying Vernon and understanding that my place was with him no matter where he was stationed, I became accustomed to traveling with him. By 36, I was an old travel and packing pro. I knew how to break down a home in a matter of hours and recreate one with just as much speed. But that lifestyle wore on me, and the sadness of leaving friends and family behind eventually took its toll. My way of dealing with grief was to ignore it and get on with the business of living. But, there is a small problem with that. When you don't release your emotions in a healthy way, they will find ways to release themselves destructively onto you. Grief wanted my life and it chose Lupus as its weapon.

In Greek, Lupus comes from the root word *lupe* as a noun, or *lupeo* as a verb. The Scriptures use this to describe being grieved or causing grief. This word also signifies pain.

No one knows why Lupus develops. Only that it is a stress-related problem that makes your immune system believe it's under attack. To save itself, the immune system creates antibodies that kill the cells needed to keep you healthy. Understand that grief is cumulative. Every time you experience a loss, your mind, soul, and body react to the pain that it feels. If grief is not properly handled, it builds up. Everyone has a "grief" capacity. Once that point is reached, grief has to be released. You may break out in hives. You may experience achy joints or an early onset of arthritis. You may repeatedly develop over 100-degree fevers. You may just be tired all the time and simply have no energy to live.

I believe the moving back and forth, and missing my family had built up over time. But it was when Vernon and I were separated for the first time in our married lives in 1988 that the stress and sadness of his absence and the death of a dear loved one soon after Vernon's departure sent me over the edge.

Vernon left to go to Greenland that September. We had never been separated as a couple. I was his traveling buddy. Where he went, I went. No questions asked. But this time, I couldn't go because this was a trip for military personnel only. Shortly after Vernon left, a dear friend of ours died of congenital heart failure. I walked with the wife through her grief process. During this period, I found myself more than empathizing with her. I found myself mourning with her. So much of our behavior was similar. I'm not talking about the crying. I'm talking about the removal of evidence that you once had a partner whom you loved as life itself.

I didn't realize how deep my grief was until the day I asked my friend if she was ready to pack her husband's clothes. She never answered me, and I didn't push. That night I went home and draped the remainder of my husband's clothes hanging in the closet with a white sheet so I wouldn't be reminded he was gone. That shook me. It made me sit up and take notice. I looked around my home and realized I had subconsciously removed every picture of Vernon from the walls, mantels, and mirrors. Just as he was physically gone, he was also spiritually gone. I acted as if he were dead.

When Vernon came back in December for a 30-day vacation, I wasn't eating. He stayed until New Year's Eve. I took him to the airport that night. The next morning, I woke up with my first symptom of Lupus — my body ached.

I wasn't properly diagnosed with Lupus until October of 1989. For 10 months I experienced unbearably achy joints, zero energy, rapid loss of weight from not eating, and rashes that left my skin blotchy. When Vernon came home for good in October and laid eyes on me, he marched me straight to a doctor.

The prognosis wasn't pretty. Doctors offered me drugs, a management plan, but no cure. I was given several prescriptions and told to stay out of the sun. Other than that, I was on my own. Here I am 36 years old and my body felt more like 80. I had just sent Vernon Jr. off to college. Layette wasn't far behind to go herself, and Jevon was only 10. All the way home from the doctor's office, I stared out the window feeling utterly overwhelmed. So, God talked to Vernon and gave him how to respond to Lupus. All I had to do was follow his lead.

Vernon stayed in prayer. I watched my husband completely take over the household plus work a 40-hour a week job. There would be days I couldn't crawl out of bed. He would work all day, help the kids with their homework, put them to bed, and then clean the house from top to bottom. I always had clean clothes and a hot meal.

When the doctors saw no cure, Vernon saw God's miracle at hand. God told Vernon to read me the Bible, anoint me with oil, pray over me, and serve me communion every day. Communion was specific: unleavened bread to remind me of the sinless body of Christ, and natural cranberry juice, to remind me of the bitter cup Jesus drank which purchased reconciliation and healing for all people. Drinking it also reminded me that my own healing was on the way. Natural cranberry juice has medicinal properties. Without sugar, the cranberry juice could cleanse my body of impurities. Sugar lessens the natural healing strength in cranberry juice.

Vernon did other things. Often some nondescript box landed on our doorstep. They would always be from natural health food stores found across the country —remedies to promote healing and convince my immune system not to attack itself. In addition to the "remedies," Vernon found ways to ensure that my life was as stress-free as possible. He encouraged me to spend time with godly friends and attend local Christian conferences. At my sickest, I looked like a modern-day leper — baldhead, raccoon face, and splotchy jet-black skin. Vernon would look past my appearance, kiss my baldhead, and call me beautiful though I felt like I was knocking on death's door.

I will forever be grateful for how Vernon honored his vow to me during my time of sickness. Only unconditional love could look past the state of my condition to see hope and beauty. Because of his love and his willingness to obey God's instruction, my hair has grown back, my face is spotless, and I've been Lupus free since 1991! Remembering his commitment to me during that season in our lives makes me fight harder to keep our marriage alive.

The power of this season forces couples to view their relationship from God's eyes. You realize that a lot of the bickering, arguing, grudges, fights, and distance you may have experienced before could have potentially short-circuited a perfectly viable and loving relationship. Life is too short for pettiness. Vernon and the children could have lost me. But because Vernon was a man of God, he knew how to go into the throne room and cry out to the Lord for help and answers. Vernon also knew how to submit and surrender to God's counsel.

More than the other seasons, the season of "in sickness and in health" brings out either the best in a person's character or the worse. Couples discover what they are made of in the thick of facing life and death situations. We watch ourselves either wilt under the pressure, or stand using the sword of the Spirit and the shield of faith. Vernon stood for me, and I am Lupus free because of it.

Facing the New Frontier Together

When a couple goes through the six seasons as one flesh, they strengthen their covenant bonds. A marriage is only as strong as the people who commit to invest in the relationship. Each season teaches couples how to commit, endure, stand, fight, pray, love, and laugh. Vernon and I have faced many a challenge and jumped those hurdles together. Yes, there were times we would stare at the challenge and look at each other as if to ask, "Do you really want to go through this one?" We'd nod, join hands, and then brave through the latest situation together.

Today, as we enter a new phase of our marriage where the children are really gone and not coming back, we look at each other with new eyes — glasses and all. He is still my calm, cool, and collected man who knows how to take charge of a situation with grace and ease. And I am still his lady full of creativity and my own brand of fire and compassion. We walk hand in hand through his mid-life experience and my menopause.

Getting older reminds me that my parents are getting older, too. I've lost my father and still find some days missing him terribly. Vernon is sensitive me and knows just when to hold my hand and let me breathe. I sometimes catch myself looking at the phone when it rings expecting to hear Daddy's familiar voice call my name. Then I wake up from my reverie realizing I'll never hear his voice again. But it's OK because I carry his memories in my heart, and his life lessons in my soul.

Mama is still here and so is Vernon's Mom. We watch them now more carefully than ever before. We've become more sensitive to their health and ours. Our best years are yet to come. We're still enjoying life; therefore, we need to ensure that our bodies will go the distance.

Lately, when we see elderly couples together I whisper to Vernon, "Baby, do you see that couple? That's going to be us in about 20 or 30 years from now." It's important to me that Vernon and I see examples of senior love because for us it means that we have much more yet to experience together. We're still running the race God set for us. It's our goal we finish the course by running it well.

Looking back through the years reminds me of Kenneth Price's book called *"The Eagle Christian."* In it, he tells the story of how eagles court. The female puts the male through a battery of tests to discover whether he would make a suitable life partner. If the male passes her tests, they take their "wedding vows" by locking their talons (feet) and turning head-over-heels in midair screaming with joy. Eagles mate for life — for better or worse, for richer or for poorer, in sickness and in health, till death to they part.

They will hunt together, nest together, raise young together, and if need be, migrate together (eagles aren't necessarily migrating birds). A change in mate happens only when there is a death. Like the eagle, Vernon and I have hunted together, nested together, raised our young together, and during his military career, moved together. When we were in high school, we got our driver's licenses together. The day we got our eyes checked, we were prescribed glasses together. I told Vernon, "Baby, we're on our way to eagle-hood."

I look forward to spending eternity with my husband, my friend. I am indeed grateful for every phase our marriage has gone through. I can say with total assurance that Vernon and I have come this far because we committed ourselves to walking the marriage covenant God's way. We committed ourselves to loving God with all our hearts, all our souls, all our strength, and all our minds. We committed ourselves to loving the Lord's people and allowing Him to use us to minister, no matter where in the world we were sent. I believe we've come this far by faith and God's grace. It's the only thing that will get any couple through the years.

Readers, when we began this journey, Vernon and I said we would share our hearts with you. It is our hopes that our lives have touched yours so your relationships with your spouses would be strengthened. It is our hope that you will take what you've learned in these pages and apply them to your lives. A lesson is only learned when you practice it. So, keep this book by your nightstand. Flip it open when you need godly counsel or just an encouragement booster. I pray that God ministers to your relationships in unique and fulfilling ways. I pray His love saturates your marriages and heals all the broken spaces. May God rekindle the love you richly deserve and may He strengthen your commitments so you too can go the distance and honor your marriage covenants in joy, peace, and everlasting love.

God bless!

"So God created man in His own image; in the image of God He created him; male and female He created them. Then God blessed them, and God said to them, 'Be fruitful and multiply; fill the earth and subdue it; have dominion over the fish of the sea, over the birds of the air, and over every living thing that moves on the earth.'" — Gen. 1:27-28

An Invitation To Accept Christ Into Your Life and Marriage

In order to experience marriage as a blessing you must first give Christ His place in your heart.

- To do this you must agree with what God say about you in the Bible.

"For God so **loved** the world that He gave His only begotten Son, that whoever believes in Him should not perish, but have eternal life" (John 3: 16).

- His Plan is that you experience abundant living.

"I came that you might have life, and that more abundantly" (John10: 10).

- Your sin separated you from God.

"For all have sinned and fall short of the glory of God" (Romans 3:23).

"For the wages of sin is death" (Romans 6:23).

- Christ paid the sin debt by dying in your place,

"But God demonstrated His love toward us, in that while we were yet sinners, Christ died for us" (Romans 5:8).

- He is the only way to God.

"Jesus said to him, I am the way the truth, and the life; no one comes to the Father, but through Me" (John 14:6).

- You must receive Christ by personal invitation. You can do so by faith and saying a prayer.

Simply say this prayer aloud:

"Lord Jesus, I need you. Thank you for dying on the cross for my sins. Please forgive me. I now open the door of my heart and receive you as my personal Savior and Lord. Thank you for forgiving my sins and giving me eternal life. Take control of my life and make me the kind of person You want me to be. In Jesus name, Amen!

If you prayed this prayer you are now born again and Christ is living in you!
I encourage you to daily pray, read your Bible and find a Bible teaching church.

Recommended Reading

Anderson, Neil T., Charles Mylander. The Christ Centered Marriage.

Arterburn, Stephen. Every Man's Battle.

Arterburn, Stephen. Every Man's Marriage. (For men)

Author, Kay. Marriage Without Regrets.

Blue, Ron. Mastering Money In Your Marriage.

Conway, Jim. When A Mate Wants Out.

Dobson, James C., Straight Talk To Men. (For men)

Eldredge, John. Wild At Heart. (For men)

Evans, Tony. A Man's Role In The Home. (For men)

George, Elizabeth. A Wife After God's Own Heart.

George. A Husband After God's Own Heart

Harley, Willard F., *His Needs Her Needs*.

Harley, Willard F., Love Busters.

Harley, Willard F., Surviving An Affair.

Johnson, Joey. God Is Greater Than… Family Mess.

Leman, Kevin, Sex Begins in the Kitchen.

Littauer, Fred and Florence. Daily Marriage Builders For Couples.

Lovett, C. S., The Compassionate Side Of Divorce.

Lovett, C. S., Unequalled Wives.

McFadden, Terri. Only A Woman.

McKinney-Hammond, Michelle. 101 Ways To Get and Keep His Attention.

Munroe, Myles. Understanding Love.

Price, Kenneth. The Eagle Christisn

Rainey, Dennis. Staying Close.

Wilson, Frank. Unmasking The Lone Ranger. (For men)

Wilson, Frank and P. Bunny. Majoring In Your Marriage.

Wright, Joyce and Norman. I'll Love You Forever.

Wright, H. N., The Marriage Check Up Questions.

Wright, H. Norman. The Other Woman In Your Marriage.

Zodhiates, Spiros. May I Divorce & Remarry?

Other Materials By Patricia Ashley

Audio Tapes/ CD/DVD

Experiencing a Fulfilled Marriage / *Tape* / *CD*
Breaking The Bondage of Anger / *Tape*/ *CD*
Key's To Life's Test / *Tape* / *DVD* / *CD*
What To Do In Your Day of Trouble / *Tape* / *DVD* / *CD*
The Woman Who Loved Much / *Tape* / *CD*
Conquering Your Giants / *Tape* / *CD*

To correspond with Patricia Ashley,
You may write to her:
c/o Ashley's Ministries
P. O. Box 6035
Moreno Valley, CA 92554-6035
E-mail her at pat@ashleyministries.org
Or log on to her website at:
www.AshleyMinistries.org

For information on booking her for a speaking engagement:
Call Vernon Ashley 1-951- 247-0174

**Look for workbook to
"Marriage Is a Blessing"
Jan. – Feb. 2005**